Disclaimer: Although the book is written in a manner to show crimes of individuals who partook in the greatest attempted coup in this country's history, no matter what is written, per the 14th Amendment of the Constitution Section 1, a person is presumed innocent until proven guilty.

CONTENTS

Introduction

To the up and coming generations, we've reached a crisis point in our nation's history. The last this severe was the Civil War when brother fought brother. Our Constitution has been brutally assaulted by forces seen and unseen. The 1st, 4th, and 5th amendment rights only apply to those who control the levers of power and not those they target and seek to destroy.

This book serves as a history lesson as our past is a guide to the present, and then to the future. In world history, there has never been a socialist country where promises made were promises kept. The picture painted is socialism leads to fairness or *"More Hope and More Change."* The reality is it never has been that way and only leaves the masses destitute, empowering a few to control all.

It's time for all to put your social media aside and pay attention to what is going on in this country as your freedoms are at stake. My one wish is that, hopefully, this book opens your eyes to what is happening to our country and the foundation of our existence, The Constitution of the United States of America with its Bill of Rights.

This book is Americana The Good, Bad, and Ugly, presented in a way that only someone who is a bit out of the ordinary can.

In my previous two books, *Dad, Why Are You So Old* and *Dad, Why Are You So Weird,* it's apparent that I enjoy making others laugh, even at my own expense.

Discovering at the age of 60 why I was so different than most others has given me a piece of mind that comes over a lifetime of being unique. My son, Jonathan, and I are focused on certain aspects of life with blinders on those things outside the sphere of our interests.

Jonathan loves everything—Transformer, eating, and irritating me. I, on the other hand, have always loved sports, have an uncanny ability with numbers that has led to making great investments in stocks and, finally, have despised those who are determined to overturn our Constitution. It is the latter that is the subject of this book. We are a nation of laws. Those who seek to subvert the Constitution have infiltrated our institutions imposing their will on the unknowing masses.

Conservative in nature, but on social issues tending liberal, I never realized how corrupt the system was until Donald Trump was elected President. With his election came an unbridled attack on the Constitution that emerged soon after he was the Republican nominee for President. Governmental powers and the mainstream media (aka MSM) have colluded to form a message that all things Trump and his supporters are racist, misogynist, homophobe, xenophobe, bigots, have no civility, and are exponential threats to our core values. They never go into detail, using only their emotions to use the President's words to twist the narrative to fit their cause.

It was Abraham Lincoln, in a speech in 1856, who said, "Actions speak louder than words." Today, 24/7 hate is all around us only because of Donald Trump's anti-globalist, anti-group think, and anti-Socialist Democracy/Communist actions the opponents to our Constitution seek to use to control our lives.

With socialism and the march to globalism and oneness, our freedom to speak out is in danger. Unfortunately, the greatest concentration of the least informed is the young people in our colleges. They have had a lifetime of indoctrination—both educationally and through the mainstream media. The fantasy of socialism sells over the reality of the numbers. Regardless of whatever you believe in, you must always look at the numbers that go behind it. If the numbers aren't true and there isn't a counter-argument to what you are looking at, chances are you are being sold a bill of goods.

With governmental control of our day to day life, we lose our individuality and freedom that goes with it. Nothing is more apparent to those paying attention that deep-rooted forces in our government caused a constitutional crisis in trying to control an election, and then via a coup d'état, unseat a duly elected President. Phony investigations were started by those who committed crimes they thought would never be discovered when Hillary Clinton was elected President. The question remains whether future generations seek to be controlled by those who seek power, wealth, and control our day to day activities by eliminating our freedom of choice, or if we still have the right of self-determination.

The common thread among socialists and deep state operatives today is Saul Alinsky. The tactics espoused in his 1971 book *Rules for Radicals* were the template for Hillary Clinton, Barack Obama, and George Soros, all from the Chicago school of Saul Alinsky, as is the old crop of socialists Elizabeth Warren and Bernie Sanders. Now, there is a whole slew of modern-day socialists including, but not limited to, Kamala Harris, Cory Booker, Pete Buttigieg, Beto O'Rourke, and Alexandria Ocasio-Cortez (aka AOC), along with a bunch of new congressional members.

With the current segment of socialists/globalists in our government, within the mainstream media, and teachers in our schools, it's difficult to escape the effect this has had on the indoctrination of a false narrative on individuals who socialists/globalists regard as "useful idiots."To the extent these anti-constitutional principles have infected our society, this is the first of two books on that disease.

This book will highlight Alinsky's 13 rules of radical tactics most effective Socialists/Globalists/Marxists/Deep State use in organizing group thought....

1. Ridicule is man's most potent weapon. (This is also my most potent weapon as you can see as you read on.)

2. Never go outside the experience of your people. (If you do, your narrative will not be understood by those you want to control.)

3. Whenever possible, go outside the expertise of the enemy. (Constantly put them on the defensive questioning them with rhetoric and emotions.)

4. Make the enemy live up to their own book of rules. (Throw at your enemy a false narrative (the means) to achieve a particular end to delegitimize your opposition.)

5. Pick the target, freeze it, personalize it, and polarize it (everything Trump).

6. The major premise for tactics is the development of operations that will maintain a constant pressure upon the opposition. (If one narrative fails, go to the next.)

7. If you push a negative hard and deep enough, it will break through into its counter side; this is based on the principle that every positive has its negative. (A particular end can be achieved with particular false means.)

8. A good tactic is one that your people enjoy. (Use ridicule to sell a false truth without having to prove anything.)

9. A tactic that drags on too long becomes a drag.

10. Keep the pressure on with different tactics and actions, and utilize all events of the period for your purpose.

11. The threat is usually more terrifying than the thing itself. (Rhetoric and emotion used effectively will make something your enemy says into something more terrifying as what you are saying needs be clothed in "moral garments.")

12. The price of a successful attack is a constructive alternative. (Destroy the rule of law, and then rebuild it into something that gives you control over the masses.)

13. The major premise for tactics is the development of operations that will maintain a constant pressure upon the opposition. (This prevents the opposition from attacking you as they are constantly on the defense.)

Within these chapters, each of the tactics of Saul Alinsky and his *Rules for Radicals* will repeatedly play out, but with a twist of irony as I will give them a dose of their own medicine in a unique and Asperger's way. Young and old alike need to know what socialism is and what deep-rooted sources in the government have done to usurp the constitutional rights of those who oppose their agenda. I urge each one of you to seek out the truth wherever it leads you and not accept anyone's words on face value. Also, remember where Alinsky-like tactics differ from the leaders of socialist/communist countries is it strikes from within and blends itself into the very fiber of our institutions. It's not done with guns, but subtly over time until it reaches the point where it's a generally accepted philosophy of controlling our thoughts.

This book serves as a bridge to the generations where references are to people long gone that the younger generation can question their elders. When talking about the current breed of rappers, parents will totally be lost. Kids will be amused to show their parents what makes them tick.

Throughout the book, I will use my son Jonathan to pose questions that every young person should be thinking about to understand what is going on in our country. Take the personal exchanges out between Jonathan and myself, as those are part of what makes Jonathan and I part of the generational struggle spelled out in our first book, *Dad, Why Are You So Old?*.

It's our individuality and ability to think for ourselves that is being threatened. When one's constitutional rights are violated, we all must take a stand against those who seek to destroy. And that's just what socialism and deep state forces planted firmly within our government seek to do. Pertaining to socialism, Ronald Reagan once said:

SOCIALISM
only works in two places:
HEAVEN where they don't need it
and HELL where they already
HAVE IT.

Chapter 1

Lessons of History and Why We Must Never Forget

Jonathan: *Dad, in our last book, Dad, Why Are You So Weird?, you raised the possibility Albert Einstein was my grandfather. Today in school, we talked about him. I told the class that he might be my grandfather. Everyone started laughing at me. Can you tell me the truth about you and Albert Einstein?*

Jonathan, this story is next to impossible to believe. But here we go. When your uncle David, the Marxist, was born on August 9, 1950, our country was in the midst of the *Red Scare*. Because of the *Red Scare*, your grandparents kept uncle David out of public viewing for years as he was a dead ringer for Karl Marx. They feared deportation to Russia.

The *Red Scare* started after World War II ended in 1945, as the Cold War between the Soviet Union and the United States intensified in the late 1940s and early 1950s. Hysteria ran rampant over the perceived threat posed by communists. This became known as the *Red Scare*.

The fear of communism led to a national witch-hunt for suspected supporters, also known as McCarthyism. Senator Joseph McCarthy (R-WI) oversaw hearings targeting suspected communists in his Army–McCarthy hearings from the late 1940s to the mid-1950s. Then, when the hearings were broadcast on television from April to June 1954, the public saw how brutal McCarthy's tactics were, much like the Salem Witch Trials in 1692. With that, the hearings ceased.

Individuals, whether rightly or wrongly, became subject to aggressive investigations before government agencies or private entity panels.

Few spoke out against it, for fear, they, themselves, would be labeled a *"Communist."*

The McCarthy era was led by Republicans. The climate of fear and repression linked to the *Red Scare* finally began to ease by the late 1950s. But the damage had been done and lives destroyed only because individuals had beliefs different from those who controlled power. The Hollywood left, and others with liberal leanings were sought out and destroyed. Examples of blacklisted individuals whose lives were decimated are many. Practically, all are gone and lost to the annals of history. But their stories should never be forgotten.

There's no story that's more heart wrenching of the consequences of the *Red Scare* than that of Paul Robeson. Robeson's father was a former slave. After obtaining a law degree from Columbia University in 1924, he appeared in two plays written by Eugene O'Neil. Robeson had an incredible baritone voice that's still present on old 78 records. He appeared in a number of movies, became an international star and an early civil rights leader. **In destroying this man's life, our government betrayed the founding fathers' declaration in our Bill of Rights.** In the 1930s, Robeson traveled to Russia and developed an affinity for its culture. He marched against Hitler and was not a supporter of Stalin's brutal tactics. He became a major spokesman against racism, in support of labor and for peace.

In September 1942, Robeson sang the National Anthem at the Moore Shipyard Workers Rally in Oakland, California.

After Robeson gave a speech in the late 1940s at the USSR-backed Paris Peace Conference, our government questioned his allegiance. It was this outspokenness and questioning the role of blacks in the military based on our country's treatment of them that finally led the House on Un-American activities to label him a *communist.* In 1950, the State Department refused to issue Robeson a passport as he declined to sign an affidavit disclaiming membership in the Communist party.

Robeson was crucified by the government for his views that destroyed his ability to earn a living as no venue in the States would want to be associated with such unpopular opinions. Leaving the States and living in Eastern Europe and traveling within Soviet Bloc countries, he eventually came back to this country in 1963. But by this time, he was in failing health due to depression and other health issues that resulted from our government's actions against him.

Paul Robeson passed away on January 23rd, 1976, in Philadelphia, Pennsylvania, the home of the Liberty Bell. In 1958, the Supreme

Court overturned the "affidavit ruling," but by then, Robeson was a broken man, both physically and mentally. Robeson was just one of many examples of government hysteria and overreach backed by the power of the United States Government used to destroy those who believed differently.

It's the people like Paul Robeson and their horrific prosecution by our government that led the way for the freedoms Bernie Sanders and Alexandria Ocasio-Cortez are granted under our 1ˢᵗ Amendment rights.

Jonathan: *Dad, how did our government get information on individuals during the Red Scare that led to prosecutions?*

The Venona Project was a counterintelligence program initiated by the United States Army's Intelligence Service in 1943, lasting to 1980. The purpose of the program was to decrypt messages transmitted by intelligence agencies of the Soviet Union. Per Wikipedia, only 3,000 messages, received between 1942 and 1945, could be decrypted. Some led to prosecutions, most notably of Julius and Ethel Rosenberg. The Rosenbergs were convicted of selling nuclear secrets to the Russians. On June 19ᵗʰ 1953, both were executed to death in an electric chair.

Although there was espionage performed by agents of the Soviet Union within our country revealed from The Venona project, destroying people's lives based on mere speculation runs counter to the Constitution, through the Bill of Rights, that protect our civil liberties.

Jonathan: *Dad, isn't the Red Scare like what is happening in the Mueller investigation? Being a public figure, who is a Trump campaign member and/or supporter, has led to the suspension of those individuals' civil rights, much like what happened in the Red Scare?*

Jonathan, there are many parallels between what happened back then to what is going on now. However, the forces who control us today are far darker and more corrupt than they have ever been. The penetration into all forms of society by elements that hate our

Constitution and the American way of life is almost complete as slowly, over time, they have infiltrated religion, media, science, law, education, health, and technology. It's the group-think mentality that seeks to silence all those who do not believe and go along. It's the Saul Alinsky tactics that are used to destroy.

But there is one paramount truth no one can dispute. I will eventually focus on only one question, and with that answer, it's obvious why those who seek to destroy our constitutional rights never sought out the person who has never been caught in a lie.

Jonathan: *Dad, why didn't I learn this in school?*

The schools these days don't talk about this *Scare.* The *Red Scare* was about Communism and Socialism coming to the United States. If you were told how bad it was, a lot of what they teach you today would be destroyed. It's in their best interest to perpetuate a narrative that Socialism is good backed by the mainstream media, as it's a way of controlling our minds on what to think. This control leads to more and more government telling us what to do and how to think.

Meanwhile, those at the top of the socialist structure not only control thought but also the financial riches that go with it. They will confiscate personal property in the name of the common good.

Socialism is based on the belief that the government is the solution for all of society's woes. With Socialism, the government decides how the means of production, distribution, and exchange should be owned or regulated by the community. In communist countries, the government has total control over all levers of society. The two are interchangeable in some ways but different in others. Both focus on equality, although it's never achieved. In a communist society, the working class owns everything, and everyone works toward the same communal goal. There are no wealthy or poor people—all are equal. And the community distributes what it produces based only on need. Nothing is obtained by working more than what is required. It inspires laziness and complacency.

Jonathan: *Dad, I like that. Do you mean I can be paid for doing nothing?*

Jonathan, you are already paid for doing nothing. It's called an allowance...and you do nothing to earn it.

Communism frequently results in low production, mass poverty, and limited advancement. Look no further than to Castro's Cuba from the late 1950s to the present day and the old Soviet Union in the 1980s. The Soviet people finally revolted, and the Soviet Union was broken up.

Jon, the dirty little secret that educators and the mainstream media do not want you to know is that neither has ever worked. There has never been a Socialist or Communist government that even comes close to surviving like our Republic (now over 230 years).

The picture Democratic Socialists paint is of a world that only exists in one other place Ronald Reagan did not mention:

Socialism/communism always breaks down as the masses are suppressed in the name of the common good. This leads to greater inequality both financially and with human rights as power is given to only a few. The leaders at the top become wealthy with the masses fighting over limited resources.

Jonathan: *Dad, why does Moe always have to appear in our books?*

Jonathan, Moe is the King of all of us, as shown in our first book, *Dad, Why Are You So Old?* It's still his world...and truthfully, whenever the Lord above says it's His time, He will forever be in our hearts and in our books.

Socialism/communism beliefs are deeply embedded in the schools, government, and mass media. Lies are commonplace, as we are constantly bombarded from all sides by individuals who want us to believe what suits them based on their biases and their desire for control, power, and wealth.

Jonathan, what's so sad and maddening at the same time is the convergence of deep state, socialism/globalism, and individuals and groups that try to sell their unfounded beliefs to destroy the very fabric of our country, The Constitution of the United States. Everything they preach has at its roots Marxism.

Jonathan: *Dad, as my education in the public schools never taught me about Marxism, what's the history?*

The history of Marxism goes back to The French Revolution in 1789 and the mass executions of the French elite. Expressing views that mirrored those of the extreme left who used terror to achieve social justice, Robespierre once said, *"Terror is nothing more than speedy, severe and inflexible justice; it is thus an emanation of virtue; it is less a principle, than a consequence of the general principle of democracy."* The old saying that *"If you live by the guillotine, you will die by the guillotine"* came true as Robespierre lost his power and with that his head.

Then with the Communist Manifesto written by Karl Marx and Fredrich Engels in 1848, **"scientific socialism"** was established. Through their political pamphlet called *The **Communist***

Manifesto (originally *Manifesto of the Communist Party*), the two German philosophers analyzed the class struggle. In doing so, they tried to debunk capitalism rather than dictating what potential forms of government they seek other than the power and control of the masses.

Scientific socialism evolved into modern-day socialism and the Alinsky tactics, where those who seek power promise everything "free " and the rich capitalist to pay. There's never a drill down to the specifics as to how to fund any of these great aspirations. It's simply platitudes with no substance. From Marx to Lenin to Stalin, their form of government sought to control the many and left with it a trail of dead in the millions and millions of their own people.

Joseph Stalin was a Marxist who was Russia's dictator from the mid-1920s until his death in 1953. Stalin's extremely brutal 30-year rule as absolute ruler of the Soviet Union—led to many atrocities, including imprisonment in labor camps, famines, torture, and mass murder. Only an estimate of between 20–60 million people murdered can be provided as Stalin was a horrible human being, and killing was commonplace. There might have been a reason for the *Red Scare*, but it was carried to the ultimate extreme.

The history of centrally-planned economies is littered with failure as nowhere in history does a socialist-mixed economy with partial nationalizations and social welfare ever work. In asking a socialist where has it worked, once they point to a Nordic country, redirect them back to California and ask what's the difference between what they are asking for and what is happening there.

The New Left in our country came about as a result of the Vietnam War in the 1960s and 1970s. At one time, these new socialists were extremely critical of the Soviet Union and were split on the type of government they wanted. The only common thought was, *"we're against the man."* The 60s radicals infiltrated **media, science, law, education, health, and technology** and wherever they could gain access to influence thought.

Then with the turn of the century, Socialism raised its ugly head as the once-thriving Venezuela was ruled by Hugo Chavez and now Nicolas Madero.

Jonathan, this now brings me to Albert Einstein. Grandpa Borovay was in a bind as he promised grandma two kids. With the fear if another boy was born, he might also look like Karl Marx or, even worse, Joseph Stalin, he reached out to Professor Einstein in the summer of 1953.

Chapter 2

Grandpa Al?

Grandpa Borovay was a very smart man, realizing he could not risk me turning out to look like a Marxist due to widespread fear that prevailed in the early 1950s. Here's a picture taken of grandpa and grandma leaving the hospital two days after uncle David was born.

In October 1953, after seeing a blurb in the *Los Angeles Times* that Albert Einstein was going to visit the West Coast to give a lecture at Caltech, he was able to track the Professor down. Calling him at his home at 112 Mercer Street in Princeton, NJ, grandpa spoke to the Professor describing in heartbreaking detail his dilemma. A normal person would have hung up on grandpa. But the Professor was so enthralled at the prospect of impregnating someone to carry on his legacy, especially someone who was not his cousin.

Finally, Albert agreed to view photos of grandma (24 at the time) and uncle David. It took 6 days to receive the photos as the United

States Post Office was the only form of delivery.

Upon receiving his mail and opening the contents to see 3-year-old uncle David, as shocked he was to see a Karl Marx lookalike, he was just as pleased to see a beautiful young lady. He was even more ecstatic that he didn't have to wear a condom and be with this gorgeous woman.

Einstein then called grandpa and arranged to come out one autumn day in 1953. It was a beautiful sunny day on Friday, October 2nd, when grandpa met the Professor at Los Angeles International Airport at 2:02pm.

At first, it was awkward for grandpa when he realized this old man was going to have an intimate relationship with his wife. That awkwardness quickly faded as he realized his next born would be a genius.

Albert, whose sense of humor is much like ours, also quickly broke the tension by saying, *"Ed, I understand your disappointment in having a son whose face only a Marxist could love. But I guarantee you that will not happen with me. My only request is to name your son, Steven Gary, after the sleigh I had growing up in Germany."*

I could go into detail on the Professor's encounter with my mother, but I do have some decency...not much. I would rather keep the legend alive than create the misconception that my father was a bit of a floozy.

As Walter Cronkite, known and polled as the *Most Trusted Man in America,* a famous CBS news broadcaster for decades, the night I was conceived stated on the *CBS News Program Up to the Minute:*

Professor Einstein departed the next day and would return the day I was born, August 8th, 1954. After holding me, Professor Einstein gave grandpa a letter. He requested that grandpa Borovay not give me the letter until I turned 30.

Here's the only known picture of my father and me together, taken the day I was born:

On August 8, 1984, my 30th birthday, Grandpa Borovay presented me with a letter that forever changed my life. Here's a copy of that letter dated August 9th, 1954:

My Dear Son, Steven:

This is your father, Albert Einstein. I know how much of a shock this must be discovering at age 30 I'm your real father. But as the saying goes, better late than never.

Although we've only met once, I want you to know we share a common bond due to our genetics. We are both Jewish and love women. I've made many mistakes with women and only ask you not to marry a relative. My Theory of Relativity was originally named the Theory of Relatives. The Science community ostracized me, accusing me of being a pervert only because I married my first cousin. I then changed the name of the theory to Relativity. I learned my lesson as such but always had an affinity for my family members.

Also, do not be wasteful with your money. Although I was a genius in science, with money, I was an idiot. Not only throwing away a ton of money to impress my lady friends, but I also went through a costly divorce and then lost my Nobel Prize money from 1921 in the 1929 stock market crash. Never place a limit on your ability to succeed and avoid people who fail to think for themselves. In life, there are only two things that are infinite: The universe and human stupidity. Whatever my beliefs are, you will be raised in a different generation. What was considered normal in my era may not be in yours. In any event, you need to find your own path to the truth as everyone's is different.

Others might view you as childlike and profoundly stubborn that comes with a purity of your spirit, much like they did me. Never give up despite the odds. It's your persistence along with your tremendous intellect that will make you a trailblazer in whatever you want to succeed at.

Finally, in 1940, when I became an American citizen, I realized how great America is. Always defend the Constitution, despite others who seek to destroy our country and our way of life. Always stand for the National Anthem! For despite all our faults, we are still the greatest nation on God's earth. Finally, always do your best to Keep America Great!

With Love,
Your Dad,
Professor Albert Einstein

Jonathan, although I was not formally diagnosed with Asperger's until I was 60, most likely Einstein had Asperger's too. Grandpa Einstein was a social outcast who felt more comfortable in his own world, left alone to follow his dreams. He had difficulty with social cues and had an intense focus on a narrow scope of topics. He had a disregard for social conventions and could care less about his appearance. With his genius, he had an incredibly spontaneous sense of humor that was not always funny to others, but funny to him. Finally, he also had a very large head that provided enough room for his very large brain. Yes, Jonathan. You and I could fit the description above almost to a "T." All this was detailed in our second book, *Dad, Why Are You So Weird?'* Asperger's explains a lot.

Unfortunately, uncle David's head is the size of a pigmy's shrunken head. Grandpa Borovay used to say to David, "A brilliant mind not used is a tragedy. But don't worry, David, this does not apply to you."

Jonathan: *Dad, did you ever take a blood test to prove Einstein is your father?*

After passing, Professor Einstein's brain was stolen prior to his cremation. There are a couple of living grandkids, but I hate to be too intrusive in anyone's life. You just need to take my word that he's your grandfather.

Jonathan: *Dad, in other words, it's "fake news"?*

Believe what you want, Jonathan. But look at his photos and those of you and me. You can see the family resemblance. In any event, whether true or not, it makes for a great story.

While Albert Einstein was visiting the United States in 1933, the appointment of Adolf Hitler as Chancellor took effect. Einstein decided he could not return to his home in Germany and as a Professor at the Berlin Academy of Sciences, where he taught physics.

Hitler was a brutal dictator with authoritarian control where central power was concentrated and political freedoms eliminated. Whether fascism, communism, socialism, authoritarianism, it's all about control by a few over the many. It's what these leaders say that goes, and no one document dictates that any citizen has a Bill of Rights.

Our country has, at its foundation, the Constitution of the United States. When the foundation is undermined, our civil liberties are destroyed.

Chapter 3

Missed It by That Much

Jonathan, back in the day when I was a kid...

Jonathan: *Dad, you're not going to talk about the dinosaurs again and your friends, Fred and Barney?*

Jonathan, stop trying to be funny as I'm trying to save our country from pure evil like Maxwell Smart (Don Adams), Agent 86 in the legendary comedy series of the 1960s, *Get Smart*. Mel Brooks and Buck Henry created a black and white version of good and evil. Smart, Agent 99 (Barbara Feldon) and the Chief (Ed Platt) worked from Washington, D.C. headquarters known as Control. As incompetent as Smart was, the good guys in the end always won.

What went on with the Obama Administration and its Deep States players only occurred because Hillary Clinton, as Maxwell Smart once brilliantly said:

What started it was the election results on November 8th, 2016, as only those whose emotion overrode logic (Sean Hannity and author, Ann Coulter) and one publication (*Investor's Business Daily*) gave Donald Trump a chance of winning.

Only about 77,000 votes from Pennsylvania by 0.7 percentage points (44,292 votes), Wisconsin by 0.7 points (22,748 votes), and Michigan by 0.2 points (10,704 votes) put Donald Trump over the top. If Clinton had won all three states, she would have won the Electoral College 278 to 260.

One of the major unsung heroes of Donald Trump's winning campaign was Brad Parscale, the digital guru of social media. The decision to campaign heavily prior to the election in these battleground states was Pascale's knowledge and Donald Trump's instincts. Pascale's brilliant mind filtered out all the negative noise around him and focused intensely on how to win a campaign that most felt was impossible to win.

Trump's victory can compare to Vin Scully's call of one of the most unlikely homeruns in World Series history in the first game of the 1988 World Series on October 15th. Vin's commentary, when a gimpy, crippled Kirk Gibson, who was more likely to be in the I.C.U. ward, let alone in a crucial moment in Game 1 of a World Series, came to the plate is legendary. With long pauses letting the crowd noise dictate the moment prior, during, and after this historic plate appearance, Scully narrates:

"And look who is coming up...

All year long, they looked to him to light the fire, and all year long, he answered the demands. Until he was physically unable to play with two bad legs, the bad left hamstring, and the swollen right knee...

With two outs, you talk about the role of the dice...this is it."

After taking A's reliever Dennis Eckersley to a 3 and 2 pitch with 2 outs in the bottom of the ninth, Scully further engrained his legend with this call:

"The tying run is on second base with two out.

Now the Dodgers don't need the muscle of Gibson, as much as a base hit. And on deck is leadoff man Steve Sax.

3-and-2. Sax waiting on deck, but the game right now is at the plate.

High fly ball into right field, she is goooooonee..."

Long pause again.

Then Vin finishes with these words:

Then, in 2016, it happened again, as against all odds, David beat Goliath. Immediately after the public inauguration, in a private ceremony, Donald Trump cited the Pledge Allegiance, but this time to the Constitution of the United States.

Then all hell broke loose in the Obama Administration, among Deep State players including heads of our Intelligence Agencies as this ceremony was spied on and celluloid film was leaked to the MSM.

After Jeff Sessions took office as Attorney General, he swore that the violator(s) of the leaked silent movie footage will be found and prosecuted. The MSM fought back against the claim it was Barack Obama who produced the film, repeatedly stating it was a Putin ally who Trump had conspired in the past with to win the 2016 election. As of this writing, there is a better chance of finding Bigfoot than bringing to justice those who leaked.

With the incompetence of Siegfried (Bernie Kopell), who was Maxwell Smart's main nemesis, and was Vice President of Public Relations and Terror for **KAOS**, those who oppose our constitutional guarantees proceeded to cover up...As President Trump would say, *"BIGLY."* Quoting Siegfried in describing who he is:

However, I will give Siegfried credit as he told you he was one of the *"bad guys."* Today, the bad guys try to come off as the good guys, as witnessed by James Comey's book, *A Higher Loyalty*. Everything that developed from the Clinton email exoneration to participating in trying to overthrow a duly elected President could have been diverted by Comey and his cohorts following one rule.... The rule of law as in our Constitution. Comey should have titled his book, *"A Higher Loyalty...to Satan."*

Jonathan: *Dad, you mean Hillary Clinton?*

Jonathan, close enough.

Now that the unthinkable has happened, the *insurance policy* former F.B.I. Agents and lovers, Peter Strzok and Lisa Page, texted each other and talked about with former Assistant FBI Director, Andrew McCabe, had to be implemented. In their minds, as Peter Strzok texted Lisa, *"Clinton should win 100,000,000 to 0."* Now they needed a diversion from crimes the Obama Administration, deep state operatives, and heads of our intelligence agencies committed to ensuring Donald Trump would never be President. All this contributed to the Mueller Special Counsel looking into something that never happened. The Mueller investigation was nothing more than colluding with those who hate Trump to obstruct justice for those who obliterated our constitutional rights. You don't have to be a rocket scientist like Wernher Von Braun to figure this out.

What was going on with the Mueller investigation into the Trump collusion with Russia was an abuse of power by those who didn't like the results of the election. More to the point, it went to hide the real corruption rooted deep in our government. A narrative has been pushed that served to weaken our Constitution and our country with it and protect those who committed crimes.

Jonathan: *Do these people even care about the laws of the country?*

Jon, it's always been about their power and control and not the rule of law. These individuals hide behind their self-righteousness in routinely violating the civil rights individuals. As Chick Hearn, the famous Lakers basketball announcer would say after a foul:

There were those who were on to it at the very beginning. In the event Clinton would have won, none of these constitutional violations would have ever come to light.

Jonathan, after researching the religious meaning of the Apocalypse, I found that there were *4 beasts in Daniel Chapter 7 of the Old Testament.* The beasts are the lion, bear, leopard, and the fourth was the most terrifying with bronze claws, large teeth, and ten horns.

From the religious site, gotquestions.org, it reads: *"The good news is that the reign of the Antichrist is limited; forty-two months, and no more. Then, God promises to judge the little horn. The court will sit, and [the little horn's] power will be taken away and completely destroyed forever"* (Daniel 7:26). *Or, as John saw it, "The beast was captured, and [was] thrown alive into the fiery lake of burning sulfur"* (Revelation 19:30). *The Son of Man will rule forever.*

So, if we count 42 months from the day Donald Trump became the 45th President of the United States on January 20, 2017, justice will be dealt out starting on July 20th, 2020. I'm not very religious, but in creating this book, I became prophetic.

Jonathan: *Dad, you are not prophetic, you're just pathetic and old.*

Geez. Forget it, Jon...

In any event, what is unbeknownst to most is that Comey and Brennan first registered to vote as Communists. Clapper is deep state rooted, and Obama, a disciple of the Saul Alinsky school of radicals.

A secret surveillance system was created during the Obama Administration led by the CIA, NSA, FBI, and DOJ to negate every American's constitutional right to privacy. The United States has turned into a police state where the federal government was weaponized against its political enemies.

At the same time, major felonies were committed by the FBI hiding Hillary's email crimes and covering for the most criminal enterprise in this country's history...the Clinton Foundation. The coverups engulfed the entire Obama Administrations and agencies who were then involved in incredible episodes of espionage against Donald Trump and his associates.

Jonathan: *Dad, is there any truth in what the MSM says about the Russian collusion?*

Jonathan, quite simply, *no*. A narrative was created after Donald Trump was elected President that he colluded with Russia to get information that led to him winning the election. With time, it has been shown the Russia collusion was on the other side of the political spectrum.

There was an incredible amount of coverage by the MSM on the Donald Trump Jr. meeting in Trump Tower on June 9th, with Russian lawyer Natalia Veselnitskaya. The purpose of the meeting was to find dirt on Hillary Clinton as revealed in emails Trump Jr, released to the public. But for Veselnitskaya, it was to focus on something else not relevant to Clinton dirt. The collusion-delusion enthusiasts could not get enough of this by trying to tie Trump Jr.'s knowledge of this meeting to his father. What was left off was never reported by MSM was Veselnitskaya met with Glenn Simpson, Founder of Fusion GPS and one of the sponsors and contributors to the Steele dossier before and after the meeting with Trump Jr... WOW! Pretty significant fact. Why disclose something that goes against the 24/7 hatred the MSM has toward Donald Trump?

After Trump won primary after primary in 2016, John Brennan, head of Obama's CIA, hated Trump with such a passion, he started an operation called, *Inter-Agency Taskforce.* Secret meetings were held with Brennan at the forefront. Peter Strzok, FBI agent, along with the National Intelligence Director, James Clapper, Bruce Ohr, 4th in command at the DOJ, met with Stephan Halper, a Republican operative. The decision was reached to have Halper embedded in the Trump campaign abroad.

In the meantime, the Department of Justice and FBI targeted two low-level Trump aides, George Papadopoulos and Carter Page. Joseph Mifsud, a Maltese professor, told George Papadopoulos he had dirt on Hillary Clinton from Russians to start the Trump-Russia Collusion scenario. Then Stephan Halper, another paid government asset, reiterated this false narrative to Papadopoulos.

It was Halper who set up a meeting between Papadopoulos and an Australian diplomat, Alexander Downer. BTW, Downer as Australia's Foreign Minister was able to get his government to contribute $25 million to the Clinton Foundation. It was Downer's tip that provided the FBI justification to start the Russia counterintelligence investigation where FISA warrants were issued to spy on Carter Page. Downer also met with Papadopoulos providing the same entrapment scheme both Mifsud and Halper used to nail him and Trump's campaign in a Trump-Russia collusion narrative.

The drill down on the level of criminal activity abroad and in our country is chilling. It would take a *War and Peace* novel to fully elaborate. Between the initial setup of Trump associates using foreign assets in Inter-Agency Taskforce, Operation *Cross-fire Hurricane* (from The Stones *Jumping Jack Flash*) started to complete and perpetuate a hoax of Russia-Trump collusion. As a Rolling Stones fan, I'm appalled, to say the least.

Chapter 4

Jumping Jack Flash and The Government Smash Our Constitutional Rights

The lyrics from the Rolling Stones song, *Jumping Jack Flash:*

> *"I was born in a cross-fire hurricane*
> *And I howled at the morning driving rain*
> *But it's all right now, in fact, it's a gas*
> *But it's all right. I'm Jumpin' Jack Flash. It's a gas, gas, gas."*

When Mick Jagger and Keith Richards were recently asked about the use of *Cross-fire Hurricane* as the Deep State moniker for interfering in the election of a President and then overthrowing of a sitting President, they responded:

I'm sure the last thing The Stones would want the people in our government to do is using a classic song as part of the most blatant political espionage campaign that we know about in our country's history.

Operatives in the governments of the U.K., Australia, Italy, and Ukraine were recruited (or attempted to be recruited and refused) to ensure a Clinton victory. The Trump Tower meeting on January 6th, 2017, between President-Elect Trump, Jim Comey, John Brennan, and James Clapper ended with Comey asking Brennan and Clapper to leave. At this point in time, Comey informed the President of the salacious dossier, and Clapper leaked to CNN that Comey was briefing the President on the Steele Dossier. It was a coordinated effort on the part of these deep state individuals to bring down a duly elected President with the assistance of the media, some of whom were awarded Pulitzer Prizes for their coverage.

Jonathan: *Dad, this appears to be a coordinated attempt to destroy President Trump. How far up did it go?*

One day after meeting with the new President, Comey met in the Oval Office with President Obama and Vice President Joe Biden to discuss how to brief Trump—a meeting attended by National Security Adviser Susan Rice, Homeland Security Secretary Jeh Johnson, Deputy Attorney General Sally Yates, and National Intelligence Director James Clapper. You look at the players here, and as the deep states' ability to withhold pertinent information deteriorates, we should be able to get to the very bottom of who. But common sense shows there was a coordinated effort to destroy that went all the way to the top of the food chain.

As such, there were those inside and outside of Government who committed multiple crimes violating the 1st, 4th, and 5th Amendment rights in the Constitution for the purpose of keeping Donald Trump from the Presidency and then afterward in destroying it.

Our 1st Amendment right has to do with religion and expression. It states, *"Congress shall make no law respecting an establishment of religion or prohibiting the free exercise thereof; or abridging the freedom of speech, or of the press; or the right of the people peaceably to assemble, and to petition the Government for a redress of grievances."*

The Fourth Amendment of the U.S. Constitution provides that *"[t]he right of the people to be secure in their persons, houses, papers, and effects, against unreasonable searches and seizures, shall not be violated, and no Warrants shall issue, but upon probable cause, supported by Oath or affirmation, and particularly describing the place to be searched, and the persons or things to be seized."*

The Fifth Amendment protects *"individuals from being forced to incriminate themselves. ... The privilege against compelled self-incrimination is defined as 'the constitutional right of a person to refuse to answer questions or otherwise give testimony against himself.'"*

With the police state tactics initiated by the Obama Administration and its officials, and with the help of Clinton surrogates, the *Steele Dossier* was spread to cover up crimes leading to the appointment of Robert Mueller to perpetuate a false narrative further. To boot, Mueller was appointed Special Counsel by another tainted bureaucrat, Rod Rosenstein, in May 2017 when Mueller and his top prosecutor (i.e., Andrew Weissmann) were aware there was no crime of collusion.

It was Rosenstein who issued the letter that fired FBI Director James Comey, then initiated the Russian-Trump collusion investigation based on Comey leaked emails by his attorney. Rosenstein also was one of the four signers to an illegal FISA warrant using the *Steel Dossier* to surveil, Carter Page, a Trump campaign associate. The investigation has more than revealed justice is no longer blind, but one-sided.

Jonathan: *Dad, some would say you hate those who hate President Trump as they are the ones who started the Russian Investigation.*

Jonathan, I hate those who try to destroy our Constitution and its Bill of Rights. We are a nation of laws. That's why I talked about the *Red Scare* initiated by the Republicans. It could have been any President, Democrat, or Republican. But we have only one Constitution. That was created in 1787, and over the years, it has been amended to correct the imperfections of the original document.

Jonathan: *Dad, why did our country permit this to happen in the first place?*

In Aldous Huxley's 1932 book, *Brave New World*, he describes a society in the future that has become dehumanized and obsessed with pleasure. That's what social media has created, instant pleasure. Whether it's social networking, microblogging, photo and/or video sharing, people spend so much time looking at social media, that their worldview is narrowed down to a screen. In the meantime, evil people are doing evil things to the basis of America, the Constitution of the United States, as most of the populace is oblivious. That's why such a crime has occurred.

Those of us paying attention, the *Open Minders*, are suffering immeasurably in our physical and mental wellbeing due to our

Orwellian nature of seeing what's really happening to our country by *Big Brother*. Also, individuals like our friend, Howard, the *Closed Minders*, are tortured by *Big Brother* stories repeated to no end in an echo chamber they use to destroy our civil liberties. The Close Minders only care about what they have been told by people they respect. Why look at the other side of the story if it destroys what you believe in? It's an Orwellian Spectrum where those in the middle can be persuaded either way to become open or closed. Those who do not fall on the Orwellian Spectrum, most of the populace, fall in the Huxley world of the Oblivions. These individuals are lost in their own social media utopia they have created for themselves. Now, it's up to the Orwellian, Open Minders, to take away the Oblivions' cell phones and smash them with the proverbial Clinton hammer.

Jonathan, you can tell if a person is lost in their own world of social media they created when the first thing they do in a new environment is finding a wi-fi connection. It's not that they are stupid. It's just that they rather be in a world they created than taking the time to see how evil people have been destroying our way of life.

Jonathan: *Dad, isn't there an old saying that ignorance is bliss?*

Not when the very fabric of our country, the Constitution and its Bill of Rights, is in jeopardy by individuals who spew a Globalist/Socialist/Marxist agenda and deep state forces who only care about their own power and wealth.

Jonathan: *How do we change the path of our country as it seems it's difficult to leave the bubble of where we are?*

Great question, Jonathan. Until some of the Closed Minders and many of those lost in their Oblivions World of Pleasure are made aware of what's transpiring and care enough to speak out, we will be lost. However, Jim Morrison of the Doors encouraged us decades ago in 1966:

Jonathan, it's a difficult battle to *break on through to the other side* as everything around us has been transformed based on false narratives, including religion, media, science, law, education, health, and technology to something that it should never be.

When one side of any argument is banned due to their beliefs, whether we agree with them are not, all our liberties are at stake. When you believe anything on face value, you are one of the *useful idiots* Alinsky values in validating a false premise.

I would rather live in a world of Aspergian's where we say what's on our mind that illustrates how we feel (and be a social outcast) than be deceiving others into believing something that was never true. Saul Alinsky was the master of persuasion and how people can be used in believing in an Alinsky-like message that gives the messenger the power to control.

Chapter 5

The Alinsky Indoctrination

Saul Alinsky was born of Russian-Jewish immigrants in 1909. Raised in a strict Orthodox Jewish family, he encountered anti-Semitism that was typical to the era. Eventually, he became agnostic. Just prior to his death in 1972, he wrote his most famous book, *Rules for Radicals*, that served as a bible for those seeking a movement for change.

Alinsky divides hu*mankind* into three groups: The *haves, the have-nots, and the have-a-little want more.* The class divide is what defines Socialism and Communism. There are many books that document this man's beliefs, but it's his *13 tactics* documented in *Rules for Radicals* that teach its followers how to control the narrative and spread social discontent. These messengers then create a new reality of there being something better under the *hope and change* mantra.

It's those at the **bottom of the totem pole, the** *have-nots,* **who are targeted by the Alinsky class warfare as they have nothing to lose.** The Robin Hood mentality of taking from the rich and giving to the poor by using his 13 tactics have been repeatedly used by the radical wing of the Democratic Party. As the Deep State tries to maintain its hold over power, despite who is in the White House, both forces are potent in their own ways. One of Alinsky's rules is *"power is not only what you have but what the enemy thinks you have."* Alinsky believed power is derived from two sources: *money and people.*

Saul Alinsky always taught and wrote to get to a particular justified end, you can justify any means if you accomplish what you were originally seeking and *clothe it in ethics.*

Jonathan, most people do not realize how they are being indoctrinated into a group-think mentality using social discontent that Socialists and the MSM pound into the society's head repeatedly to control the narrative.

In politics, MSM stands for Militant Socialist Movement. In media, MSM stands for Mainstream Media. Ninety percent of the televised media is controlled by six enormous entities owned by GE, News Corp, Disney, Viacom, Time Warner, and CBS. News Corp owns Fox News and is the exception to the group-think mentality of the other outlets. As per repeated surveys by polling outfits, Trump's negative rating on Fox is 52 percent, while on other MSM outlets, the negative ratings are over 90 percent on all stories connected to his name. Although Fox is considered part of the 90 percent of media reach, it's viewed by many as an alternative to the group-think logic of other outlets. Fox News, for the most part, tolerates opposite views, while MSM fires those who go over their lines.

The biggest victim of groupthink is now the majority of those who attend college. They are the most fertile for new ideas and fall within the definition of what Alinsky would have called *useful idiots*. They are the very definition of *have-nots* as numerous students are mortgaged to the hilt with student debt. Their minds are fertile for cultivation into a Socialist/Marxist philosophy that has never worked.

In part II of this Alinsky series, I will show the lies kids are told where Socialism becomes an accepted alternative in their safe space world of fairness and social justice. The kicker is they are never told where these principles originate.

Furthermore, nothing has ever been mentioned by the MSM about Obama's origins and how his roots go back to Saul Alinsky. It was only the detractors on the other side who would disclose his dark past and roots in Alinsky's Marxist-like tactics. There has always been a liberal bias in newscasts and newspapers, but never more apparent than today. When public figures such as Obama and Clinton have had to hide their socialist values, today's current crop of Marxists flaunts them.

One of Alinsky's most effective tools in organizing group thought was *ridicule is man's most potent weapon*. While Barack Obama was the master of humiliating the other side, Donald Trump took it to another level and could be among the Greek Gods on Mount Olympus. Hopefully, someday I can be among them. As you can tell by now, I think I use it pretty effectively to get a point across and, more importantly, to divert people's attention away from their electronic devices. My hope is, someday, they will be in the Orwellian world of the Open Minders to see what's really transpired in our country that is a threat to all who believe in the Constitution.

There was never any justification to start the Mueller Special Counsel into Trump-Russia collusion as a crime would have had to be committed to initiate it.

Chapter 6

Deep State Operatives

Instead of investigating the real crimes, a DNC, Fusion GPS and Hillary Clinton funded dossier through the law firm, Perkins Coie, a Mueller Special Counsel investigation was started to violate the constitutional rights of individuals only because these individuals supported Trump and were mentioned in the fictitious *Steele Dossier.*

FISA (Foreign Intelligence Surveillance Act) warrants were obtained by the top brass at the FBI and DOJ through the courts based on unverified and ludicrous contents of the Dossier. MSM, deep state operatives, and politicians repeated parts to no end to give it credibility.

Edward Bernay, an Austrian-American pioneer in the field of public relations and propaganda, was later known as the *father of public relations.* One of his uncles was Sigmund Freud. In his 1928 book *Propaganda* he wrote:

"The conscious and intelligent manipulation of the organized habits and opinions of the masses is an important element in a democratic society. Those who manipulate this unseen mechanism of society constitute an invisible government which is the true ruling power of our country. We are governed, our minds are molded, our tastes formed, and our ideas suggested, largely by men we have never heard of.... It is they who pull the wires that control the public mind."

The truth is if Russian collusion was even the issue that caused interference in our election and Hillary Clinton to lose, why didn't the Mueller team question or charge Julian Assange? It was WikiLeaks that disclosed damaging contents of the Clinton collusion with the DNC and the Podesta emails showing their underbelly of corruption and deceit. Why was Mueller's 18 investigators Hillary and/or

Obama supporters handpicked by Robert Mueller/Andrew Weissmann for their bias against Donald Trump?

Weissmann is well known for his strong-armed tactics that led to the accounting firm, Arthur Andersen, shutting down. Over 80,000 individuals lost their jobs over made-up crimes involving Andersen in the Enron collapse by Weissmann and his prosecutors in the DOJ. Later, after lives were destroyed, the Supreme Court overturned 9–0 the crimes the lower courts ruled against Andersen's top staff. Sydney Powell's book *Licensed to Lie* documents crimes by our government in prosecuting Merrill Lynch executives for non-crimes and provides the basis of how the government's unlimited power can destroy lives unjustifiably due to its bad actors.

Andrew Weissmann was at the Hillary Clinton convention center ready to celebrate her Presidential victory on November 8th, 2016, and it didn't happen. Those who followed the activities of the Special Counsel based on prosecutorial tactics thought Andrew Weissmann was leading the charge and not Robert Mueller. With the Congressional Hearing held as Mueller, the only witness on July 24th, 2019, this was confirmed. Mueller revealed how hands-off he was in the investigation, depending on Weissmann to lead the witch hunt started by Rod Rosenstein.

Jeannie Rhee represented the fictitious 501(C3), known as the Clinton Foundation, in a racketeering case in 2015 in a lawsuit that claimed the Clinton Foundation operated as a racketeering enterprise shaking down donors in exchange for official favors. The lawsuit was dismissed. She then served as the Deputy Assistant General in the Obama Administration and was Hillary Clinton's attorney in a lawsuit seeking blocking release of the Clinton emails. Mueller admitted during the July 24th, 2019, Congressional hearing he was not made aware Rhee represented Hillary on her email scandal until after Weissmann retained her services. Despite this major conflict, Rhee remained on until the end of the investigation. Wow! Talk about the fox minding the henhouse!

That's the story behind only two of the chosen. You only must ask one question to understand that this team was put together under the presumption of guilt of Trump and his associates. The question that remains is if you're looking at a crime, why don't you start at the lead up to the crime. These people with heavy Clinton and Obama ties never cared about equal justice for all.

Here is a picture of Mueller's 18 prosecutors:

Former FBI agents (and lovers) Peter Strzok and Lisa Page were given the boot by Mueller months after their text messages to each other revealed their tremendous hate toward Trump.

Jonathan: *Dad, how did Mueller get away with hiring partisan hacks?*

Jonathan, the system of checks and balances collapsed. An illusion was perpetrated that was played to the nth degree, never focusing on the true criminals from within. You must remember too that Mueller wasn't even leading the investigation and was just a figurehead to give it credibility.

Andrew Weissmann was the one pulling the strings on everything that involved bringing President Trump and his associates down. It doesn't absolve Robert Mueller of anything as people's lives were destroyed as a result of an investigation that should not have taken place, to begin with.

The Democrats have a history of marching in lockstep to their party leaders. The Republican establishment funded primarily by the big establishment donors permeates throughout Washington D.C. and would like nothing more to see Donald Trump booted out of office.

The State of the District of Columbia hates Donald Trump, too. He received the lowest total (4.09 percent) of the vote of any Presidential nominee in recorded history. As all forces colluded to start an investigation into Russian collusion with Trump and his campaign associates and supporters, our constitutional rights have been tossed aside. Many think we are in a post-constitutional era.

The truth is justice was never the issue with Mueller with his 18 anti-Trump, pro-Hillary, and Obama prosecutors who have been entrenched in our system for years (deep state to the core).

Mueller charged two individuals, Paul Manafort and Michael Cohen, with past crimes that had nothing to do with Trump and Russia collusion. The other crimes, for the most part, were process crimes brought by Mueller and his team of marauders.

The funny thing about the Manafort indictment, one of the individuals given immunity was Tony Podesta, brother of Clinton's lead advisor, John Podesta. Strangely, both Manafort and Podesta did deals with Ukraine together. Why was Podesta granted immunity, and it was not the other way around? After all, the Podesta Group, formed by Tony and John, was implicated with Manafort in illegal Ukrainian activities at the start of the Mueller investigation. The reason why is that Podesta equals Clinton and innocence in the minds of the prosecutors.

The facts came out later that the FBI was targeting Manafort earlier than when he became part of the Trump campaign for foreign dealings. This was despite the fact that the FBI shut down an investigation into Manafort back in 2014. As per the *Hill's* John Solomon, the document used was the unverified *Black Cash Ledger* from a Ukrainian source that was used by the FBI to obtain warrants on Paul Manafort.

Jonathan, I don't want to go into detail on why Manafort was charged, but not Podesta, other than to say again equal justice was never a priority of Mueller and his investigative team. Unfortunately for Manafort, he would never have been part of any investigation if he had not been part of the Trump campaign.

Then, Mueller's team came up with charges against 13 Russian individuals who worked with 3 Russian companies in Russia. Mueller/Weissmann knew they would never appear in a U.S. court. However, to their surprise, one of those accused came forward with his attorney requesting disclosure of evidence used in coming up with the charges. To date, Mueller and his team have stalled to no end, failing to produce any evidence that this individual was involved in colluding with Trump to sway the election against Hillary Clinton. The reason why? It never happened.

Again, if justice was what Robert Mueller was seeking, why didn't he file charges against Julian Assange, WikiLeaks founder, and the source of the leaks? To understand why, you need to understand Mueller's deep state roots.

After 9/11, the Bush Administration dragged us into a war in Iraq based on potentially false government intelligence information on WMDs. BTW, one of the main cover-up leaders was the then FBI Director, Robert Mueller. Back then, most of us believed there was a threat that Iraq had *weapons of mass destruction,* and they were going to *develop nuclear weapons.* It was the repeated theme of Bush Administration officials to justify us in invading Iraq. But was it based on information from false governmental agency reports?

In retrospect, as the facts slowly came out, **it appears we were misled by our government based on inaccurate deep state information resulting from the relationship that President Eisenhower referred to as the *militaristic-industrial complex.*** Unfortunately, that's what big government does without us knowing. Bureaucrats firmly implanted within our government, unelected officials, do not have the proper checks and balances to be held accountable, and as such, the public is scammed.

Robert Mueller and James Comey have a history of crony capitalism. When Mueller was FBI Director, he gave Lockheed Martin a large FBI security contract. It just so happened that Comey was hired as head of security with no cyber background and paid over $6 million in one year. Then when Comey was FBI Director, Mueller was a partner in a law firm that received a multi-million dollar contract from Comey's FBI.

Supporters of Mueller and his investigation henchmen point to the fact he is a registered Republican. I point to the fact Mueller is deep state to the core. The acts he performed of overreach and unjustifiably destroying people's lives had more to do with his power and control than any political bias. Whether it was under the Bush or Obama Administration, he typifies what is wrong with our country.

No further proof of his deep state nature is needed than when Mueller came out on May 29th, 2019, with a press conference announcing his retirement from the Justice Department. At the conclusion, he stated he will no longer further comment on his report, *as it speaks for itself.*

During the July 24th, 2019 Congressional hearing, when Mueller was forced to speak, it was obvious that he was only the poster boy of justice. Weissmann used Deep State Bob to give the investigation a disguise of creditability needed to perpetuate a false narrative against the President and his associates. As many of Weissmann's appointees worked in the Obama Justice Department, who better to cover up crimes than those who were a part of them? It's the old axiom, *a good offense is a good defense.* If Mueller is out there casting doubt on those who did nothing, the crimes of his persecutors go unchallenged.

However, as a dog is twice as smart as a cat, the dog knows to follow the one controlling the flashlight, while the cat is so enthralled with the light, the cat follows the light wherever it goes.

Fortunately for all of us, there are enough dogs out there to keep the pressure up and ensure justice is finally brought.

A narrow focus is needed as those who control us always defer, deflect, and point the finger at someone else. Sometimes, they deny, deny, deny before deferring. Many times, they refuse to deny as the truth is so obvious and create a phony scenario to support their arguments. The only crime for many of those convicted by Mueller and his band of Constitutional Obstructionists was process crimes and being a public figure who supported Donald Trump.

Just ask Roger Stone.

Chapter 7

When Your Only Crime Is Who You Support for President

Roger Stone is the Rona Barrett of the modern era. Barrett was a Hollywood gossip columnist in the 1960s and 1970s. Stone, 66 at the time of his arrest for process crimes involving tampering, obstruction, and perjury in the Mueller investigation, has been a political operative dating back to the 1970s. All these charges were brought after the Mueller investigation started and only because Stone was a close ally of Trump for decades. Roger Stone is about as harmless as one could be. Yet, the pre-dawn raid on January 25th, 2019, with 29 FBI agents and 13 FBI vehicles, had Stone being taken off in handcuffs. He's been charged with a political crime.

As the *Boston Herald* reports: *"After his arraignment on witness tampering, obstruction, and lying to Congress, a rattled Stone was quoted saying 29 agents 'pounded on the door, pointed automatic weapons at him, and terrorized his wife and dogs.' Stone was taken away in handcuffs, the sixth associate of President Trump to be indicted in Special Counsel Robert Mueller's probe into Russian meddling in the 2016 election. All the charges have been related to either lying or tax evasion, with no evidence of so-called 'collusion' with Russia emerging to date."*

The irony of the arrest was Stone's ties to WikiLeaks and Julian Assange. Those who followed the facts knew that Roger Stone has about as much chance of contacting and influencing Julian Assange to release damaging information pertaining to Hillary Clinton as a socialist looking out for the common good and using the truth to justify their ends. This doesn't happen in the real world. For Robert Mueller and his team of hooligans, it was about destroying and unseating a duly elected President and hiding crimes of those involved in the prior administration and multitudes of other deep state figures.

The repeated violation of the civil rights of individuals had no bounds in the Mueller investigation. Jerome Corsi, a conservative author, was dragged into the interrogation due to his connection to Stone. Corsi is an anti-establishment author casting assertions against the far left and the establishment mainstream Republicans.

On the premise of the bogus story that Stone had direct contact with Julian Assange and knew of the leaks prior to WikiLeaks releasing, the special counsel sought to destroy Stone's life to perpetuate the false narrative they had created.

Jonathan, Julian Assange, who has never been disproved, came out and said he never had any contact with Roger Stone and that Stone has been trolling democrats his whole public life. When you study Julian Assange and how he operates, he doesn't have backchannels to preannounce information he's about to release. Assange comes out in advance with general information providing a ballpark date as to the disbursement of information.

The fact the Mueller team has never questioned him or disproved what he says feeds into their argument that Trump's allies are guilty. Then the MSM, instead of exposing the truth that doesn't fit their narrative, pound into the viewers' minds the crimes of Paul Manafort and Michael Cohen and try to tie them to Donald Trump.

It's a vicious cycle as the special counsel had no problem in dragging individuals who have reputations as *flame throwers* and others based on allegations with no proof of Trump-Russia collusion. For an individual without unlimited wealth to go against the deep pockets of the United States government is a losing battle that results in mentally, physically, and financially breaking that individual into, as Professor of Law, Emeritus, Harvard Law School, Alan Dershowitz says, *singing and composing.* It's always been a mere distraction from the truth. It's never been about what's good for the country but taking out a sitting President by whatever means possible.

For if it was about the truth, Julian Assange would have already been granted immunity from prosecution and allowed to testify.

Chapter 8

MSM and the Perpetuation of Lies and Hate

The MSM had a love affair with Barack Obama, resulting in holding back and failing to show his true roots and criticism of his policies. Hiding his past didn't fit the narrative created by those who got him elected.

The MSM still has failed to ask him about his 2005 photo with Louis Farrakhan that was hidden from public view until after he left office? It all made sense spending 20 years in a house of worship with Reverend Wright and his spew of hatred for our country and his friendship with Obama.

A simple question from the media is, how should a Jew feel about you having taken a picture with the most notorious Jew-hater in the world? And the media response...crickets. With the current composition of Congress with House members who openly display their hatred for Jewish people and the State of Israel, it's no surprise why there isn't the outrage when hatred for Jews has run so rampant. Neither the Democrats, establishment Republicans, nor the MSM calls out this blatant hatred. Instead, uninformed or Jewish hating people elect officials that detest Jews or Christians only because of their faith.

As a Jew, I would only be in a photo with this man under two conditions. One, I'm dead or two, he's dead. But a smiling Obama with the number one Jew-hater in the world is inexplicable. Where are you the socialists/ globalists, human rights lovers in the Democrat party, the MSM, or the Hollywood left to express your outrage? If it doesn't fit your narrative, you are silent, and it never happened.

The four ring leaders of the new voice on the far left have a hatred for our country and that of Israel. With that hatred comes their belief that the Constitution needs to be destroyed in favor of something where they can control us using their rhetoric and emotion.

These women would equate this photo of Netanyahu and Trump together, much like Jewish people would of Obama and Farrakhan together.

Ask someone you know which photo they find more reprehensible. If they say they don't know who all four people are, they are one of the Oblivions and need to pay more attention as the Four Horsewomen want to take away our constitutional rights. If they say the Trump/Netanyahu photo is more deplorable, they are no fans of Jews and cater to the rise of Anti-Semitism globally. If they refuse to answer, chances are they are doing it to be politically correct in their world. In the mind of an Aspie, I'm able to separate good from bad as facts prevail over emotions.

Jonathan, when I posed the question to uncle David to explain the Obama-Farrakhan photo, like most far-left socialists, he defers, deflects, and points his finger at someone else. Because he has no answers! The question literally speaks for itself with the truth self-evident. But I will defend to no end Farrakhan's right to express his views however hateful they are.

When questioning uncle David why Obama would even appear in a photo with this man, he went to the *"well, Donald Trump referred to the incident at Charlottesville, South Carolina, as there are good people on both sides."* The fact that there were radicals on the left and radicals on the right (KKK) doesn't mean there weren't people there who believed that the Robert E. Lee statue should remain as it tells us about our history. Tearing down the past just because it's no longer *socially acceptable* is wrong, as we tend to forget. That's what Socialism/Globalism does as it wants to take our history away from us, and we become all the same.

So, in uncle David's mind, I'm a white Nationalist instead of just a Nationalist who thinks America comes first. I guess if I was one of the protestors saying the Lee statue should remain, then I'm not a good person. It's what the radicals do—condemnation of anyone and everyone who holds different views.

Very little is heard from the MSM and others about how the radical arm of the Democratic Party has confiscated the narrative with their anti-Semitic views that are spreading around the globe. Not only Jews, but Christians are also a targeted group, especially within the Middle East. There is a cultural genocide of Christians that few media outlets cover in this country.

Instead of censuring those in Congress such as Congress lady, Ilhan Omar's continual anti-Semitic remarks, uncle David avoids condemnation and talks about something else with pure emotion. It's difficult to argue with this type of irrational thinking, but I realize years of marijuana abuse has crippled whatever mental capacity he would have left due to normal aging.

Jon, but the fact remained, uncle David wouldn't even address why Obama took a smiley face photo with the leading anti-Semite in the world. Add to the fact this photo was hidden from public view until after Obama left the Presidency. So much for his words of *hope and change.* Why has no one held Obama accountable for appearing with Farrakhan, who compares Jews to termites?

Jonathan: *Dad, is the rise of socialism related to the rise in anti-Semitism?*

Jonathan, everything is interrelated as the hatred of Jews is part of the Globalism/Socialist/Marxist movement. Israel stands out alone as a Democracy in a sea of kings, dictators, and others who rule with an iron fist. One of the leaders of this movement, Billionaire and activist George Soros, is a Hungarian Jew who worked in a concentration camp doing what the Nazis asked him to do to survive. He hates Jews and the state of Israel as has become typical of some of the new members of Congress. The photo of Obama and Farrakhan together would have been unacceptable back when Obama first ran for President. However, members of the black caucus in Congress have no problem meeting with Farrakhan. It's a hatred that's growing rapidly within our society.

In the April 25ᵗʰ, 2019 edition of the *NY Times International*, a cartoon appeared portraying Israel Prime Minister, Benjamin Netanyahu, as a dog with President Trump holding his leash wearing a Yarmulke. This, much like words, are not actions. The real-life version of Obama's action of going to meet and then smile in a photo with Farrakhan shows a deep-seated hatred for Jews that supporters of Obama at most will only pass on as a *mistake.*

Why are Jewish members in Congress including Reps Adam Schiff and Jerold Nadler and Senators Richard Blumenthal and Charles Schumer more concerned in participating in a coup of a duly elected President with a hoax of Russian collusion, than combatting real hatred of members in their own party? These individuals make public statements and issue letters of condemnation. But it's merely a manufactured outrage as there is no follow-up to the blatant anti-Semitism exhibited by some members of Congress. It's a form of righteous indignation, only symbolic in that they spoke up.

When questioning a very wise lady who loves this country and Israel, she stated that as many Jews have Eastern European roots, it's difficult to speak out against the socialist mantra their parents and grandparents grew up under.

But why are not people on both sides of the isle forming the Jewish Caucus to combat the blatant anti-Semitism we see on the rise in this country? As these acts continue, why is there no active coalition within Congress that pushes back the way the haters push their narrative on Jews and Israel forward? Hatred against any one segment of the population needs to be called out for what it is.

When watching the Don Lemon broadcast on CNN on May 13th, 2019, he covered the rise of anti-Semitism in the United States, blaming it on White Nationalists' exposure on social media as the leading cause. Nowhere does he state the blatant anti-Semitism within Congress. It doesn't fit the narrative, so why cover it as it only exists when you expose it?

Jonathan, the scary part, is Barack Obama's vision of the future. From Zerohedge.com and a Washington Examiner article speaking at the Bell MTS Place in Canada in March 2019 speech, **Obama** explained, "*If we could form a network of those young leaders, not just in the United States, but around the world, then we got something. If we can train a million Baracks and Michelles who are running around thinking they can change the world, they will fulfill the 'hope and change' agenda.*"

This is a repeated theme as Obama will never stop indoctrinating those who are most vulnerable, making Saul Alinsky smile from beyond the grave.

Defectors from the MSM come out from time to time with the truth about the networks they worked for. In a Mike Drop Podcast interview on February 15th, 2019, conducted by retired Navy Seal, Mike Ritland, Laura Logan, a former CBS News 60 Minute correspondent, stated journalists have *"become political activists."*

In the interview, Logan explains: *"Eighty-five percent of journalists are registered Democrats. How do you know you're being lied to? How do you know you're being manipulated? How do you know there's something not right with the coverage? When they simplify it all (and), there's no gray. It's all one way. Well, life isn't like that. If it doesn't match real life, it's probably not. Something's wrong. For example, all the coverage on Trump all the time is negative.... That's distortion of the way things go in real life."*

Further, Logan stated, *"We've abandoned our pretense—or at least the effort-to be objective, today.... We've have become political activists, and some could argue propagandists, and there's some merit to that."*

Laura Logan believes, ***"The responsibility for fake news begins with us."*** Finally, saying that when the MSM using anonymous or single government sources, *"That's not journalism, it's horseshit."*

Jonathan: *Dad, if the MSM continually perpetuates lies about the Trump-Russian collusion and obstruction, how will we ever get to the truth?*

Jon, it starts with one man but goes through another.

Chapter 9

The Real Rocket Man and The Real Journalist

Wernher von Braun worked in Nazi Germany's rocket development program during World War II and became America's first Rocket Man.

Per The NASA.Gov website, it's written:

"Dr. Wernher von Braun (1912–1977) was one of the most important rocket developers and champions of space exploration in the twentieth century. As a means of furthering his desire to build large and capable rockets, in late 1932, he went to work for the German army to develop liquid-fuel rockets. Based on his Army-funded research, von Braun received a doctorate in physics on July 27, 1934.

After 1937, von Braun and his scientists worked at a secret laboratory at Peenemünde on the Baltic coast. A liquid-propellant missile, 46 feet in length, and weighing 27,000 pounds, the V-2 flew at speeds in excess of 3,500 miles per hour and delivered a 2,200-pound warhead to a target 200 miles away. First successfully launched in October 1942, it was employed against targets in Western Europe beginning in September 1944. The V-2 assembly plant at the Mittelwerk, near the Mittelbau-Dora concentration camp, used slave labor, as did several other production sites. Von Braun was a member of the Nazi Party and an SS officer. Yet, he was also arrested by the Gestapo in 1944 for careless remarks he made about the war and the rocket. His responsibility for the crimes connected to rocket production is controversial.

By late 1944, it was obvious to von Braun that Germany would be destroyed and occupied, and he began planning for the postwar era. Before the Allied capture of the V-2 Rocket Complex, von Braun was sent south, eventually to Bavaria and surrendered to the Americans there, along with other key team leaders. For fifteen years after World War II, von Braun worked with the U.S. Army in the development of ballistic missiles. As part of a military operation called Project Paperclip, he and an initial group of about 125 were sent to America, where they were installed at Fort Bliss, Texas. There they worked on rockets for the U.S. Army and assisted in V-2 launches at White Sands Proving Ground, New Mexico.

Von Braun also became one of the most prominent advocates for space exploration in the United States during the 1950s, writing numerous books and several articles for magazines such as Collier's. Von Braun also served as a spokesman for three Walt Disney television programs on space travel, Man in Space.

In 1960, President Eisenhower transferred his rocket development center at Redstone Arsenal from the Army to the newly established National Aeronautics and Space Administration (NASA). Its primary objective was to develop giant Saturn rockets. Accordingly, von Braun became director of NASA's Marshall Space Flight Center and the chief architect of the Saturn V launch vehicle, the super booster that would propel Americans to the Moon. At Marshall, the group continued work on the Redstone-Mercury, the rocket that sent the first American astronaut, Alan Shepard, on a suborbital flight on May 5, 1961. Shortly after Shepard's successful flight, President John F. Kennedy challenged America to send a man to the Moon by the end of the decade. With the July 20, 1969 moon landing, the Apollo 11 mission fulfilled both Kennedy's mission and Dr. Von Braun's lifelong dream."

What was left out in the NASA bio was that the rockets he helped to design in WWII were used in the latter part of the war and launched in Paris, London, and Antwerp that killed both citizens and allied troops. In the bio, it only refers to *targets.*

Jonathan: *I thought Kim Jung Un or Elton John was the first rocket man?*

Jon, Kim Jong Un was *Little Rocket Man,* but Un was born in 1984—long after we landed on the moon. Elton John wrote *Rocket Man* that was released in 1972. At von Braun's funeral on June 16th, 1977, in a private ceremony at Ivy Hill Cemetery in Alexandria, Virginia, Elton John bid his farewell to this legendary figure by singing that iconic song. Later in the ceremony, David Bowie finished the sendoff by singing his classic, *"Ground Control to Major Tom."*

History is our lesson, and you never want to delete the negative as it's a lesson that all should know about and not repeat or rewrite if it's obliterated.

So, however you view Julian Assange, it's an unequivocal fact that Wernher von Braun was at one time an enemy to the United States and became one of the major forces in the NASA space program that brought us to the moon. There's been an incredible amount of misinformation spread about Assange purposely to feed a narrative that he's an enemy of the U.S..

The irony in both their stories is the **NASA** connection with Julian Assange hacking the **NASA** database at age 18 in 1989. However, by 1989, von Braun was dead and remains dead to this day.

It's impossible for an ordinary citizen to sort out the facts from the lies. But the truth starts with the individual who holds the golden key in unlocking the Mueller Russian investigation into President Trump, campaign associates, and his supporters. A silent coup d'état has occurred where Obama Administration officials, going all the way to the top, fueled by the Clinton cabal weaponized our government to take down candidate Trump, President-Elect Trump, and then President Trump. The Russians had nothing to do with Trump being elected President.

Per Justice Louis D. Brandeis, *"Publicity is justly commended as a remedy for social and industrial diseases. Sunlight is said to be the best of disinfectants; electric light the most efficient policeman."*

There's always a motive as to why people do the things that they do. In Assange's case, it isn't for money. As of the time of this writing, his net worth is only $1.3 million. That's not to say, because of his tech background, there might be bitcoins hidden somewhere. Truthfully, it wouldn't fit the narrative of someone who searches for the truth that big government hides from their citizenry. There are very few people on this planet who have enough conviction to place their values over monetary interests. Just ask the Clintons or Bernie Sanders (with his four houses).

Jonathan: *Then, why wasn't Assange granted immunity and allowed to testify to what he knows?*

Some people view Assange as a hero while others as a criminal. Mike Pompeo, when he was Trump's CIA Director, at the Center for Strategic and International Studies on April 13th, 2017 stated:

"That is one of the many reasons why we at CIA find the celebration of entities like WikiLeaks to be both perplexing and deeply troubling. Because while we do our best to quietly collect information on those who pose very real threats to our country, individuals such as Julian Assange and Edward Snowden seek to use that information to make a name for themselves. If they make a splash, they care nothing about the lives they put at risk or the damage they cause to national security.

WikiLeaks walks like a hostile intelligence service and talks like a hostile intelligence service. It has encouraged its followers to find jobs at the CIA in order to obtain intelligence. It directed Chelsea Manning in her theft of specific secret information. And it overwhelmingly focuses on the United States, while seeking support from anti-democratic countries and organizations.

It is time to call out WikiLeaks for what it really is—a non-state hostile intelligence service often abetted by state actors like Russia. In January of this year, our Intelligence Community determined that Russian military intelligence—the GRU—had used WikiLeaks to release data of U.S. victims that the GRU had obtained through cyber operations against the Democratic National Committee. And the report also found that Russia's primary propaganda outlet, RT, has actively collaborated with WikiLeaks."

But here's the real story as told by John Solomon of *The Hill* in a January 22ⁿᵈ, 2019 article: *"As it became clear during the 2016 U.S. election that Donald Trump had a mountain of support underneath him, nervous Democrats connected to the Hillary Clinton camp reached out to U.S. officials over a half-dozen times, each tapping a political connection to get suspect evidence into FBI counterintelligence agents' hands."*

So even the former CIA Director, now Secretary of State, Mike Pompeo, was misled. Where's the proof? Other than words, it has never been shown publicly. **The Trump-Russia narrative was promoted through the Obama Administration, State Department, Congress, Justice Department, the CIA, the FBI, and foreign intelligence assets. It started as an obvious political campaign to smear an opponent to win an election. Then, when Donald Trump became President, a silent coup d'état became a reality as hostile forces used a *fake dossier* to diminish and remove President Trump.**

Chapter 10

Julian Assange – The Truth Seeker and the George Washington of Journalism

In today's environment, much like the 1940s and 1950s *Red Scare*, collaborative forces throw out an untruth, and those who are attacked are left to defend something that has never happened. It's like when someone asks, *when did you stop beating your wife?* The fact that you have never beaten your wife is no defense. When it's repeated countless times by the forces that influence your thinking, it's even more lethal. For now, a lie has become a truth.

Jonathan, it doesn't matter what President Trump does or says as he truly gets no respect. It probably started from birth.

Rodney was incredible! An era when funny was funny, and it didn't matter your race, religion, creed, etc. It was just pure humor.

Jon, remember the time your teacher told the class that President Trump—because he was against illegal immigration—was trying to overturn the 14th amendment?

Jonathan: *You told me that she did it to show what an evil person Trump was.*

Your teacher never told the class that she felt President Trump raised the possibility that kids of illegal parents born on our soil may not have the rights of naturally born citizenship. She never explained he raised the possibility only, and that no action has been taken against those individuals whose parents are illegal to the country whose children are born on our soil. Furthermore, she never told the class what it would take to overturn a Constitutional Amendment. The Constitution's Article V requires that an amendment be proposed by two-thirds of the House and Senate or by a constitutional convention called for by two-thirds of the state legislatures. It is up to the states to approve a new amendment, with three-quarters of the states voting to ratify it. In other words, it was never going to happen. The teacher knew that and only said that to spread the emotion of hate about the man and what she thinks he represents.

A lot of Americans believe in what the President does. He stands for the Constitution and the Rule of Law. Although unconventional in his methods of going around those who hate, using social media to get his unfiltered message across, whether you like him or not, he doesn't leave it up to individuals or organizations that hate him to distort his message. That alone ticks them off to no end as it runs counter to those who have broken the law in holding their power and influence. It stands against socialism, globalization, groupthink, open borders, and free stuff for the less privileged that's needed to hold control over the populace.

Julian Assange believes the public, the ordinary citizen, has a right to know about illegal activities of its most powerful and how governmental power is exercised by those who could care less about anyone but themselves.

Jonathan: *Dad, tell me more about Julian Assange as he seems to be a defender of our first amendment rights of freedom of speech.*

Assange was a computer programmer who, at a young age, hacked in the NASA system. He founded the media organization WikiLeaks in 2006 and practices what he calls "*scientific journalism.*" In his publication, he provides source material provided by others with minimal to no editorial commentary. Assange, through WikiLeaks, released thousands of internal and classified documents from an assortment of government and corporate entities. He has never been found to publish any false documentation and is the go-to source in exposing corruption at the highest levels of government in numerous countries.

WikiLeaks' international website gives whistleblowers anonymity needed to release sensitive documents. For without this, they could be arrested for stealing or even killed.

From Wikipedia: *"On 16 August 2012, Foreign Minister Patiño announced that Ecuador in London was granting Assange political asylum because of the threat represented by the United States secret investigation against him and several calls for assassination from many American politicians. There were charges of sexual malfeasance that were later withdrawn by the Australian government. He has stayed in the embassy as there are extradition threats to the United States that started under the Obama Administration and have continued under the Trump Administration. The crime he would be charged is treason under the espionage act punishable by death.*

"WikiLeaks revealed through DNC emails that the Clinton campaign subverted the DNC using its power to ensure Bernie Sanders would not be elected. The leaked contents suggested the party's leadership had worked to sabotage Bernie Sanders's presidential campaign. Then with the John Podesta emails, Hillary Clinton's lead campaign advisor, some of the emails provide some insight

about the internal conflicts of the Clinton Foundation, revealing pay-for-play when she was Secretary of State through speeches former President Bill Clinton gave for outrageous fees."

Sometimes, I use Wikipedia as a source of information I've vetted through other outlets. Jonathan, in any event, never take anything from anyone on face value if it's important to fit a narrative.

Also, pay-for-play means Hillary Clinton made promises to provide foreign entities or private citizens certain political favors for donations to the Clinton Foundation and/or speaking fees. Multiple potential felonies have been detailed in several books with the paper trail extremely convincing. A thorough audit of the Clinton Foundation showing fraud was performed by Charles Ortel. Ortel is the one who exposed crimes committed by AIG and GE. He's also nonpartisan.

Quite a contrast between Jimmy Carter after his presidency of being a key spokesman for Habitat for Humanity and the incredible work done by that organization versus the Clinton Foundation. Strange, you never hear from those who supposedly benefitted from the Clinton Foundation's generosity.

The audit trail in reading numerous articles and books is so thorough that it's difficult to believe our system of justice failed so miserably that the Clintons have never been held accountable.

The WikiLeaks releases along with FBI Director James Comey, re-opening the investigation on Clinton emails just prior to November 2016, could have cost Clinton the election.

On the eve of the 2016 Presidential election, Assange released a statement in which he declared no *"personal desire to influence the outcome,"* noting that he never received documents from the Trump campaign to publish. He explained, *"Irrespective of the outcome of the 2016 U.S. Presidential election, the real victor is the U.S. public, which is better informed as a result of our work."*

The biggest WikiLeaks scandal prior to this one involved Chelsea Manning, a former United States Army soldier who was convicted by court-martial in July 2013 for violations of the Espionage Act and other offenses. WikiLeaks disclosed nearly three-quarters of a million classified or unclassified but sensitive, military and diplomatic documents. Manning was imprisoned between 2010 and 2017. Some of the videos provided by Manning released by WikiLeaks showed U.S. soldiers killing innocent citizens in Iraq via drone.

Eventually, President Obama commuted the sentence, and Manning was released. Originally named Bradley Manning, he had a sex-change operation and changed his name to Chelsea.

Jonathan: *Dad, what does Manning sex-change operation have any-thing to do with what you're talking about?*

Nothing, Jonathan. It just makes this book more interesting. Personally, I like her after picture better than his before one. I would date her if she wasn't a man prior.

The scandals due to the release of governmental documents in the name of free speech are not prosecutable as WikiLeaks is merely publishing online information that was provided to them. Our government is trying to extradite Assange based on phony charges that he helped Manning in gaining access to sensitive military documents. However, there is no legal basis (although I'm not an attorney) for him being convicted.

There is precedence for what Julian Assange has done without criminal prosecution. In 1973, Daniel Ellsberg, an American activist and former United States Military analyst who, while employed by the RAND Corporation (an American nonprofit global policy think tank that provided the United States Armed Forces research and analysis), released top-secret documents relating to the Vietnam War. These papers later became known as *The Pentagon Papers.* The insights provided showed that our government had knowledge that the war as then resourced could most likely not be won, and the Johnson Administration knew this as it lied to Congress.

In January 1973, Ellsberg was charged under the Espionage Act of 1917, along with other charges of theft and conspiracy, carrying a total maximum sentence of 115 years. Due to governmental misconduct and illegal evidence-gathering, the judge dismissed all charges against Ellsberg in May 1973.

The criminality of the Deep State and those supporting them are revealed through WikiLeaks and others who believe in our right to know what the government is doing. Only through technological innovation has secrets those in power wish to hide have been revealed. Major technology players, including Google, Twitter, and Facebook, along with the MSM, have no problem suppressing the truth and hiding the sins of their Deep State benefactors. If it doesn't fit the narrative of groupthink and runs counter to the Socialist/Globalist utopia, they do not want you to hear or read it. For, in the world they created, if it's not reported on, it never happened.

The establishment now openly suppresses the truth by ignoring it and making issues of things that divert your attention from the real issues. Those who differed and stated there is no Trump-Russia collusion were ridiculed and, for the most part, ignored. Why bring something to your attention if it runs counter to your narrative? The level of hate I see in this country, I've never witnessed in my lifetime. Julian Assange needs to be heard as the purveyors of hate will be destroyed.

Jonathan, I took this passage out of the Encyclopedia Britannica on Julian Assange: *"In 2016, Assange became an active player in the U.S. presidential race, when WikiLeaks began publishing internal communications from the Democratic Party the campaign of Democratic candidate Hillary Clinton. Assange made no secret of his personal hostility toward Clinton, and the leaks were clearly timed to do maximum damage to her campaign. Numerous independent cybersecurity experts and U.S. law enforcement agencies confirmed that the data had been obtained by hackers associated with Russian intelligence agencies. Despite this evidence, Assange denied that the information had come from Russia. In January 2017, a declassified U.S. intelligence report stated that Assange and WikiLeaks had been key parts of a sophisticated hybrid warfare campaign orchestrated by Russia against the United States. In May 2017, as Assange approached his fifth year under de facto house arrest in the Ecuadoran embassy in London, Swedish prosecutors announced that they had discontinued their investigation into the rape charges against him."*

Numerous publications—that were once reputable—got it 100 percent wrong. Who knows what to believe? In the article, it cites U.S. law enforcement agencies confirmed that Russian intelligence agencies hacked the Democratic Party and Hillary Clinton. The most infamous independent cybersecurity experts were *CrowdStrike*. The DNC and its head, Debbie Wasserman Schultz, refused to turn the hacked server over to the FBI. Instead, *CrowdStrike*, a heavily connected Democratic-backed company, was the only one to be granted access. Without producing any evidence to suggest collusion with Russia, *CrowdStrike* came out with a report that Russia operatives hacked the DNC computer. No evidence was ever produced. Only the words of a politically- biased company were repeated throughout the mainstream media. There was no word about attorney Marc Elias whose law firm, Perkins Coie, funded Fusion GPS (a source of funds for the *Steele Dossier*) and hired CrowdStrike to do a forensic analysis of the DNC server. Also, Britannica's reference to U.S. law enforcement agencies doesn't tell the reader that there were originally 17 intelligence agencies that eventually ended up with only 3 (including the Coast Guard).

Encyclopedia Britannica left out the fact that the greatest silent *coup d'état* in our nation's history was based on a document that had no basis in reality. **A Clinton and DNC funded opposition research report produced by a former British spy, Christopher Steele, known as the *Steele Dossier*, fabricated a fairytale that neither its author nor those who pushed it as authenticated ever verified. Additionally, Steele's hatred of Trump has been well documented.**

Encyclopedia Britannica only discredited Julian Assange's repeated statement that all WikiLeaks information on the DNC and John

Podesta did not come from Russia. He's never been proven wrong. There was no re-writing of the piece. This is how they do it. They throw out a false narrative as the truth but never produce direct evidence to prove Julian Assange wrong. It's a repeated theme through the mainstream media, politicians, and those who hate President Trump. No facts, only rhetoric and emotion.

Jonathan: *Dad, why is the MSM trying to undermine a sitting President?*

Jonathan, these people are against President Trump's actions that run counter to the globalist, socialist, and groupthink mentality they seek to change our Republic to Socialism. Also, there are those on the right, who have vast fortunes at stake that they could be affected by closed border policies. Their businesses thrive on cheap, illegal labor. These individuals and groups spew groupthink to achieve their objectives. The swamp in D.C. is so deep, and thanks to the MSM contribution, it's difficult for the average Joe and Josie to see the forest from the trees.

Chapter 11

The Fairy Tale Called the *Steele Dossier*

Jonathan: *Dad, what was in the dossier that was so salacious and untrue?*

Very little was true, other than what was already out in public. Carter Page, a Trump campaign associate, traveled to Russia and did some work there. But who in their right mind would believe something that even its creator, Christopher Steele, couldn't prove and only created it because of his admitted hatred for Trump (and for money)? Four FISA Warrants were issued on Carter Page based on the Dossier. No charges were ever brought on Page whose Constitutional Rights were violated repeatedly, as there was never any justification to have spied on him in the first place. The irony of everything prior to putting Carter Page under surveillance was Page assisted our government for many years. He provided information to the FBI that served in part as the basis for charging Russian operatives, Sporyshev and Podobnyy, in 2013 with conspiracy to violate the Foreign Agents Registration Act. Now, he was being used by some of the same forces he was allied with and surveilled to find a *crime* only because he was on Donald Trump's side.

There's one part of the *dossier* where Donald Trump was caught on video by Russian operatives in 2013 at the Moscow Ritz Carlton with prostitutes who were urinating on a bed that President Obama and Michelle had slept on during their visit to Moscow:

Here's the passage in the Steele Dossier:

"3. However, there were other aspects to TRUMP's engagement with the Russian authorities. One which had borne fruit for them was to exploit TRUMP'S personal obsessions and sexual perversion in order to obtain suitable 'kompromat' (compromising material)

on him. According to Source D, where s/he had been present, TRUMP's (perverted) conduct in Moscow included hiring the presidential suite of the Ritz Carlton Hotel, where he knew President and Mrs. OBAMA (whom he hated) had stayed on one of their official trips to Russia and defiling the bed where they had slept by employing a number of prostitutes to perform a 'golden showers' (urination) show in front of him. The hotel was known to be under FSB control with microphones and concealed cameras in all the main rooms to record anything they wanted to.

4. The Moscow Ritz who said that s/he and several of the staff were aware of it at the time and subsequently. S/he believed it had happened in 2013. Source E provided an introduction for a company ethnic Russian operative to Source F, a female staffer at the hotel when TRUMP had stayed there, who also confirmed the story. Speaking separately in June 2016, Source B (the former top-level Russian intelligence officer) asserted that TRUMP's unorthodox behavior in Russia over the years had provided the authorities there with enough embarrassing material on the now Republican presidential candidate to be able to blackmail him if they so wished."

And here's the picture they took:

Jonathan: *Dad, that's outrageous and impossible to believe that anyone with one brain cell would even try to pass it off as legitimate! Who would be stupid enough to believe this crap?*

The same people would belief this who would buy this bridge.

As Moe is taking the votes, Tia, your trainer, and you are counting them, and I'm in the background separating the highest ones.

Karl, my friend, was in shock that a former President would even talk to him that way. Additionally, he was puzzled as to why Obama knew to pronounce his first name with a *K* instead of a *C* most people would say.

I then had to sit my friend of over 40 years down and explain why: *"Karl, as I'm a writer supporting Constitutional law and my grandparents on my father's side are from Russia, the Obama administration through their deep state connections had a FISA warrant issued by the court to surveil me. You were collateral damage as the former President needed to know what was going on. As such, you were illegally unmasked by Samantha Powers, former UN Ambassador."*

Karl, like the true patriot he is, responded, *"I have no problem taking it for our country. However, these people need to pay for their crimes."*

Jonathan: *Dad, why is our friend's Howard stomach in the illustration?*

To his credit or detriment, Howard is the only one for the past couple of years who is willing to engage me in civil conversation. He has only the CNN, MSNBC, and MSM view of President Trump and 2 minutes a week he watches alternative outlets to get the other side of the story. Ninety-eight percent of Howard's dislike of President Trump comes from what he's heard as the MSM pundits express outrage over their interpretation of Trump's words. It's rare that Howard can cite any Presidential action that goes against our Constitutional Rights. Words to him, like a lot of others, mean more than actions.

On the Trump Tower meeting, it was obviously collusion in Howard's mind between Donald Trump Jr. and Russia for dirt on Hillary. I asked him about the *Russian* attorney who met before and after this meeting with Glenn Simpson, Founder of Fusion GPS, and one of the funders of the Steele Dossier. He questioned who Glenn Simpson was. Obviously, the only 2 minutes of the other side of the story was never factored into my good friend's logic. In his mind, as in many others, who cares about the facts and what Walter Cronkite said was needed to get to the truth.

It's sort of like when Neville Chamberlain, Prime Minister of the UK, negotiated peace with Adolph Hitler, stating in a September 30th, 1938 speech, *"We have peace in our time."* The believers in *words mean more than actions* rejoiced. Obviously, history dictated otherwise.

Jonathan: *Dad, why does Howard even try to argue with you using no facts?*

Jon, look at the size of his stomach. To get him to partake in these revealing discussions of the other side (Close Minders), I fed him well...too well. Also, other than me, Howard tries to count his brother as a friend. I won that argument, as his brother, Dennis, was forced by their mother to be Howard's friend after he was born in 1957.

Despite the heated telephone conversations, we constantly have, if I was Howard, I would have hung up the phone on me long ago. I can be very irritating and focus on a narrow range of topics. Howard's a great CPA and should stick to what he knows. Bottom line: he's one of my few friends over the decades who constantly has my back. Hard to find in my life as there are multitudes who took that knife and stabbed me in the back.

Anyway, back to the long single-file line for the London Bridge that goes for a couple of thousand miles with Roger Daltrey of the Who singing....

Jonathan: *Dad, why is Saul Alinsky's ghost in the picture?*

Democrats have a long history of having dead people vote. Back in 1960, John Kennedy questionably won Illinois on the back of Chicago Mayor Richard J. Daley. Chicago is famous for its history of people voting from the grave. John F. Kennedy beat Richard Nixon by 9,000 votes in Illinois by capturing what some considered a suspiciously high 450,000 advantage in Cook County. Daily's political machine is well documented in books as he was Saul Alinsky personified. However, both were on opposites sides of the power dynamics. Daley supported those in power with corruption, while Alinsky sought out those the system oppressed, the minorities.

After counting the ballots for bids on the bridge, there were 65,844,954. Incredible coincidence as that was the number of votes Hillary got in the 2016 election. The sad fact is her voters first had the choice of voting for a nominee who was not so corrupt. The second sad fact is that they didn't have to vote at all in the Presidential election. These people lacked common sense as instead of forming multiple lines, they lined up single file. When they hit the Atlantic Ocean, they tried to form a human bridge to Normandy, France. Alexandria Ocasio-Cortez was so proud of these people as she stood at the dock in Atlantic City shouting through a megaphone:

But as the Clinton supporters were brainlessly jumping into the ocean, a straight line of over 20 million people suddenly turned around and no longer were listening to Ocasio-Cortez. Instead, these individuals realized they were being controlled by idiots and had thoughts about getting both sides of the story before committing to ending their lives. The formerly Closed Minders and Oblivions used rational thinking asking one simple question...What sacrifices have Hillary Clinton or any of these Alinskyites made for us in return for the power and control we've given them over the decades?

America this time didn't have to storm the beaches of Normandy to save our Democracy. Additionally, some of the deplorables who drowned were caught by fishermen in nets and later used to feed the starving populations of third-world countries. Finally, Hillary did the world some good!

My conversation with Karl concluded with him saying, *"These people are morons! I can understand someone wanting to own a bridge. It's like owning a Tesla. It gives you prestige. But what in God's name would anyone want to own that bridge? Especially because everyone knows London Bridge is falling down"*.

Even though the top people in our intelligence agencies were aware that the dossier had no basis in truth, it didn't matter as everything had to be done to stop Donald Trump.

Jonathan, there are a lot of misinformed and emotionally misdirected people who can be manipulated by the MSM, social media, the Democratic Party, and establishment Republicans that hate Trump. They lack the ability to reason and see what a coup attempt was from the very get-go.

Yet a **DNC, Fusion GPS, and Hillary Clinton funded dossier through the law firm Perkins Coie became the center of the greatest political espionage act in our country's history. Then the Mueller Report only served to further discredit Donald Trump by not investigating the individuals responsible for perpetrating a hoax.**

Those who hate Trump and our Constitution had no problem in spreading it. Had Hillary Clinton won the election, none of this information would have come to light. So, many on both sides of the political spectrum got it wrong.

But whether he's an enemy or friend, **Julian Assange knows the truth about who were the sources of the WikiLeaks documents exposing DNC and Hillary Clinton's corruption.** The truth is Assange is not an agent of any country and acts to provide citizens what they need to know about their leaders. That fact alone makes it dangerous in our time to expose those people who are still controlling the levers of power.

If Assange is an enemy, Wernher von Braun set the precedence in bringing a former enemy in the country to help us reach for the stars.

Chapter 12

The Mueller Investigation and Deep State Continued Attempts to Destroy Our Country

On March 24th, 2019, after 672 days of investigation and over $32 million spent of our taxpayer dollars, Robert Mueller and his team found no collusion. Attorney General, Bill Barr, and Assistant General, Rod Rosenstein, then found no obstruction. The Collusion Obstruction Delusion bubble exploded, as no one in their right mind could dispute the findings. Barr's synopsis of findings had *"Mueller's team working with 40 FBI agents, intelligence analysts, forensic accountants, and other professional staff. The Special Counsel's office issued more than 2,800 subpoenas, executed nearly 500 search warrants, obtained more than 230 orders for communication records, issued almost 50 orders authorizing use of pen registers, made 13 requests to foreign governments for evidence, and interviewed approximately 500 witnesses ."*.

Despite the unlimited financial resources at Mueller's disposal and political opponents to President Trump as part of the special counsel leaving no stone unturned, the Russian–Trump hoax was finally exposed as the walls of Jericho came tumbling down.

The sad part of the whole collusion matter was the individual who knew the source of *'Russian Collusion'* WikiLeaks founder, Julian Assange, was never called to testify. Furthermore, the Steele Dossier and its perpetrators were never investigated. Remember, the truth was never the subject of the Mueller Investigation. The truth was one those in power never wanted to come out. With the kill the messenger mentality, Assange is viewed by the Deep State as a traitor. This would be apparent to anyone who set aside their emotions and looks at both sides of the story.

Investigations in Mueller Special Counsel were based on the Steele Dossier and never acknowledged as such in Mueller's report. The last thing the Mueller report would shine light on is the Obama Administration and Clinton allies who would do anything to ensure Trump was not elected President.

After all, these same individuals did anything to ensure they were not caught performing major crimes against the United States. Mueller's pit bull, Andrew Weissman, hired individuals who would only continue to cast a shadow on President Trump. The deep state used Alinsky tactics. In this case, it's keep the pressure on, with different tactics and actions, and utilize all events of the period for your purpose.

Going from one false narrative to another, whether it be collusion to obstruction to treason to whatever the purpose for the MSM and deep state is to keep the public's focus on Trump and never direct it toward themselves.

Jonathan, it was always so simple. But hatred runs deep for President Trump, and the deflection from the truth was nothing but to conceal crimes committed by those who have no sense of law and order. The omissions as to why in the Mueller Special Counsel investigations started in the first place into George Papadopoulos, Carter Page, Lt. General Flynn, and all the Trump allies targeted is called a paper trail, and it's nowhere to be found in Mueller's report.

Nowhere in the Mueller Report is mentioned Stephan Halper, a paid Obama Administration informant, only Carter Page, who served our intelligence agencies over several years for free as he truly loved this country. It just goes to show you the old saying, *crime doesn't pay* was never not truer.

Australian Ambassador, Alexander Downer, who assisted Obama Administration officials in setting up individuals within the Trump campaign was also not mentioned. BTW, Downer arranged a $25 million contribution from Australia to the Clinton Foundation. And where is Azra Turk mentioned who was part of the initial contacts in the setup of Trump associates in the Mueller report? Turk was a

CIA operative working with the Turkish government. Nowhere in the Mueller report does it spell out this whole operation started in Ukraine with the Obama and Clinton people seeking to get dirt on Paul Manafort to pollute Trump's campaign.

It wouldn't fit the narrative if Mueller reported the truth on how this corrupt special counsel started in the first place. The individuals listed above were paid by our government to spy on political opponents through the Obama Administration.

Tragically, Julian Assange's arrest was timed, so he would remain silent on the allegations in the Mueller Report. Assange stated numerous times his sources were not from Russian or those with Russian affiliations, DC Leaks, or any of the Russian connections Mueller lists as contacts to Assange. Factoring Assange has never been found wrong. It's horrific that he's silenced just prior to the release of the report. Assange's arrest was brought about after the meeting between Vice President Pence and the Ecuadorian Ambassador. Debt relief to the tune of $4.2 billion dollars was given by the U.S. to Ecuador in exchange for the arrest of Assange by the U.K. police.

Conspicuously absent in the Mueller report was any email or direct links to the DC Leaks, Gucifer 2.0, or the GRU to Assange. Additionally, as the DNC refused to turn over their server to the FBI during the investigation, the FBI instead relied on a DNC ally, CrowdStrike, to analyze who hacked into the system. The Mueller report fails to state where CrowdStrike got their information from. The report acknowledges that no hardware devices of the DNC or John Podesta were even inspected by the special counsel or their hires. Why would anyone trust a source, CrowdStrike, that has ties to the Clinton network, including its attorney, Marc Elias (who was a Clinton Foundation and DNC attorney)?

Delaying the release of the final report to after the November 2018 elections was another tactic by Mueller, through individuals like Andrew Weissmann, to keep the MSM and political hacks busy in saying there was *substantial proof* Trump colluded and obstructed. Although knowing by then, there was no crime, Mueller and his team were able to influence the outcome by ensuring the Democrats took the House over from the Republicans.

Remember, too, Jeannie Rhee was both on the Mueller team and a Clinton Foundation attorney and handled Hillary's email scandal. The drill down on those involved in investigating Trump and his associates on the other side is so disturbing, the question remains how could something like this happen in our country.

The crimes of the DNC, including its one-time head, Wasserman-Schultz, using their power structure to ensure Hillary was the nominee to this date, have not been fully investigated. Why was the target, Bernie Sanders, quiet when the proof came out that the DNC blocked Sanders from any possible win? I guess if you're on the right side, you can't complain too much, especially as it would hinder any further attempt by Bernie to be the party's next nominee.

It's all common sense, and if you're only looking at one side of the story, either because you hate Trump or are just plain ignorant, it was when darkness came to light that the greatest political scandal in the history of our country was shockingly revealed. To those who saw the truth from the outset, none of what came out was a surprise. Remember, always being the dog and look at the one holding the flashlight and not the cat following the light.

It's always the who, what, where, why, and how that tells a story is what constitutes the basic ingredients of any well-told story. Mueller conveniently leaves out the *how* in the story. How did the Mueller investigation even start when there was no evidence of collusion? It's the *how* of the story that shows *why* Mueller's team selected certain individuals to be swept up in an investigation that never was based on reality. The fact that the prime driver of the investigation into Trump and his associates, The Steele Dossier and its author, Christopher Steele, were never mentioned shows how individuals mentioned in the Mueller report were the subjects of a bogus investigation into something that never happened.

Why not charge and investigate the individual responsible, Julian Assange, who published this information stolen from the DNC and John Podesta's emails? Common sense.

What's the purpose of finding the truth when it doesn't fit your narrative? Alinsky until the end...a particular means justifies a particular end... As no criminal activity could be found on Donald Trump's part, what better way than divert the public from the truth by creating phony crimes and finding past crimes of those who were allies, although they had nothing to do with Donald Trump? This masquerade covered up the tracks, temporarily, of those who knew they violated the constitutional rights of our fellow Americans. Instead, the innuendoes on Trump's obstruction were thrown out in the second part of the Mueller Report to continue the witch hunt that had no basis to begin in the first place.

The sycophants will maintain President Trump's guilt on anything despite no evidence to the contrary. An Alinsky tactic of diversion—by deflecting, blaming someone else and not answering questions that point to the truth—has been used repeatedly by those who hate. Emotions prevail over logic.

Chris Hedges, former *New York Times* foreign correspondent, stated that *cultural schizophrenia* promulgated by the U.S. media is tearing the country apart. Based on a RAND study of news media from 1987 to 2017, the media has evolved from content and context-based reporting to advocacy and emotions based appeals, I.e., the truth no longer matters.

The question remains why were the investigation and order for the Special Counsel by Rod Rosenstein mandated in the first place when there was no crime, to begin with?

What was not so shocking was that Head of the Intelligence Committee, Adam Schiff, still maintained after the release of the Mueller Report that Trump colluded using the meeting his son Donald Jr. and other top Trump campaign officials had with Russian attorney, Natalia Veselnitskaya, on June 9th, 2016 to obtain *dirt* on Hillary Clinton. Of course, Schiff failed to mention that this Russian attorney met with Fusion GPS (i.e., Steele Dossier) funder and contributor, Glenn Simpson, prior to the Trump Tower meeting and afterward.

Jonathan: *Dad, why are the findings still being disputed? That's just stupid!*

As that famous American, Forrest Gump, once said: *"Stupid is, as stupid does."*

Chapter 13

A Banana Republic and Coup from Within

In one of Woody Allen's early movies, *Bananas (c.1971),* Allen, as Fielding Mellish, was involved in a revolution in the fictional country of San Marcos to overthrow a sitting President in a coup d'état. After the leader's demise, his nose was placed in cold storage awaiting cloning. Mellish took the nose of the former leader, then threw it in front of a steam roller. The movie and coup were funny.

Then there was the Obama led coup:

That coup was TRAGIC!

Jonathan: ***Dad, you've repeatedly used the term a coup d'état.*** *What is that?*

Jonathan, **it's an illegal and overt attempt by the military or other elites within the state apparatus to unseat the sitting executive.** In this case, high-level FBI, DOJ, CIA, State Department, and officials in the Obama Executive Branch, including President Obama, have decided Trump was not qualified to run for President. So, they launched illegal investigations for no legitimate reason. In the process, violations of individuals' 1st, 4th, and 5th amendment rights were commonplace.

What transpired involved so many people and countries that only a Jerry Bruckheimer (of CSI and movie producer fame) could present accurately what happened. **It's the Nixon Administration's low-level crimes versus crimes of sedition and treason of the Obama Administration and Deep State intelligence agencies heads in the Trump** *coup d'état.*

Without Trump's election, we would have never known the levels of corruption deep within our institutions and governmental bodies perpetuated by the mainstream media that despises this President.

It's sad that the checks and balances established with our Constitution have been thoroughly abandoned. Now those who bear contempt for our Constitution speak out against it without much push back. Socialism has infiltrated our society and attacked our most precious commodity—our youth.

Jonathan: *Dad, why didn't the checks and balances work?*

In this case, the Attorney General of the United States could have prevented what transpired with the Russian Investigation into President Trump and his associates only by doing his job.

Edwin Burke, an Irish political philosopher and Whit politician in the 1700s, allegedly said, *"All that is necessary for the triumph of evil is that good men do nothing."* Unfortunately, that is what happened as the one man in charge of overseeing corruption, Jeff Sessions, failed to act.

Jeff Sessions was nominated as Attorney General by President Trump and confirmed by the Senate on February 8th, 2017, and sworn in on February 9th, 2017. Immediately after being sworn in, Jeff Sessions recused himself from the investigation into Russian interference by the Trump campaign due to his participation in supporting Trump during the election and meeting with a Russian Ambassador.

Whether this was the right or wrong decision, Sessions failed to disclose this to the President prior to accepting the position. That was wrong. Also, blame President Trump as he has hired several individuals at key positions who haven't served their country faithfully. In his defense, who would have known the level of corruption or stupidity embedded deep within our institutions? How politicized these bodies have become is beyond anything I would have ever imagined.

What transpired after President Trump was duly elected has led to
the greatest internal *coup d'état* in our country's history. Individuals
involved in the Mueller investigation, including the former Assistant
Attorney General, Rod Rosenstein, have potentially committed
more crimes than those they are pursuing.

Jonathan, I don't want to go into too much detail here as there are
a few best-selling books that document what transpired. At the end
of this book, I will give references and praise to those who got it and
understood the corruption of those involved.

For those that know what really transpired, Jeff Sessions will go
down as the Benedict Arnold of this generation.

Sessions took an oath as Attorney General that he never lived up to,
and we have all suffered as a result.

Jeff Sessions can be compared to another historical figure, Nero.
Nero fiddled away while Rome was burning, while Sessions fiddled
away while our Constitution was being set on fire.

The level of disgust I have toward both parties makes it difficult to understand why anyone would ever be associated with either the Democrat or Republican party. There should be a party known as the Commonsense Party, as neither side seems to have a grasp of reality.

It's difficult to say why Sessions removed himself from all investigations, including the leaking of confidential information and surveillance of Trump, campaign associates, and his supporters by Obama Administration personnel, FBI, DOJ, and former heads of major government institutions including former heads of the C.I.A., John Brennan, and National Intelligence Director, James Clapper. Instead, Sessions appointed surrogates to investigate crimes within his jurisdiction that further delayed and denied justice to the real criminals. What was exposed by the MSM was the narrative they spelled out, which had very little to do with the truth.

Jonathan: *Dad, was Sessions deep state too? Or did those who control our government have some damaging information about him. Or was he just plain stupid?*

Jonathan, I have my suspicions:

It became obvious that Sessions was over his head after the Obama Administration's IRS Scandal targeting filings of conservative political 501(C)) (3) and 501(C)(4) from 2010 to 2012 for tax-exempt status. The DOJ's decision was not to prosecute those in the government who violated the 1st amendment rights of the political action groups. Instead, the DOJ, through Jeff Sessions, issued an apology and paid a $3.5 million settlement (roughly $14,000 per litigant). It was obvious from that point on that Jeff Sessions wasn't going to rock the boat. The biggest outrage was Lois Lerner, the former head of the Tax-Exempt Division who pleaded the 5th at targeting groups, retired and is now living off a government pension.

Like the Hillary Clinton email investigation, hard drives with evidence of IRS criminality were destroyed with no other consequences than the loss of a job, but with full retirement benefits. It was beyond any logic. Many involved in the current coup have left their positions within government either being fired or willingly leaving knowing that benefits, including a pension, await despite their misdeeds.

Currently, only Andrew McCabe was stopped from serving to the point he would have earned a pension. What does he do then? He sues the government for wrongful termination based on the

1ˢᵗAmendment! CNN then hires him on as a Contributor. Much like McCabe's Go Fund Me page, CNN continues his funding because they like his narrative of Trump hate. It's a common thread among networks that hate Donald Trump to employ individuals who have potentially committed crimes against our country and its Constitution, including John Brennan (former CIA Director) and James Clapper (former National Intelligence Director). It makes an ordinary citizen who follows the law physically sick as individuals who subverted our Constitution are rewarded.

Four years after misdeeds occurred, the perpetrators, like Andrew McCabe, have been emboldened as the two-tier system of justice continues. As of this writing, former and current government employees who have leaked confidential information have not been prosecuted. Individuals have had their lives destroyed over crimes that were created by the opposition still in power at the time Obama was President. If the leakers are government employees, so far nothing to worry about. If, on the other side of that paradox, someone misremembers an unimportant part of their statements to law enforcement, they are prosecuted. No wonder those paying attention to both sides of the story are stunned to the core seeing that if justice is not rightly served equally, the Constitutional Rights of all Americans only apply to those in power and their ilk.

However, I truly believe with Jeff Sessions, it was the Peter Principle that applied. This principle, as it applies to Sessions, is that most government employees rise through the bureaucracy to a level where, in the end, they show incompetence. Sessions was a pretty good Senator and a very nice man. Hopefully, he runs again as Senator from Alabama because that was his calling.

It seems to be the common thread of coverups during the Obama Administration. Hillary's secret email server was known to all, including President Obama (who emailed Clinton under an alias), his Attorney General Lynch who blocked legitimate investigations, and those who pushed the collusion delusion (Congressmen Adam Schiff and Jerald Nadler and Senator Mark Warner among many others). It's how this government under Obama worked and a reason why big government without proper checks and balances can give untethered power to a select few. These individuals used our tax dollars to pursue crimes against their political enemies.

So, what transpires after this bogus report comes out? More useless and costly investigations by government executed in Gestapo- like precision to take the enemy out. Not only a 1-sided investigation, but now multiple investigations into looking for crimes come as a result. That means more of our tax dollars and printed money going down the proverbial toilet. The big government just prints more money with no profit motive.

Saul Alinsky tactics of pushing a *false narrative* repeatedly until it's a *fact,* then ridiculing those who care to dispute it was commonplace during the Obama Administration.

It brings me to the question, why would anyone want the federal government to control anything other than matters concerning our national safety? It's about centralization with no accountability and bureaucrats determining policies and procedures without proper monitoring. That's insane! Whether it's health care, education, providing entitlements to keep able-bodied individuals from work- ing, it just doesn't work.

Again, it all goes down to typical groupthink that does nothing more than verify anything with emotion instead of facts. The problem with groupthink is the constant mantra of words that ring throughout the MSM such as *"constitutional crisis, cover-up, impeachment, ob- struction, unhinged, chaos, the walls are closing in, tipping point, going to resign, reminds me of Nixon's last days, bombshell, break- ing news...it's the end of Trump, etc. "*that become engrained in our minds as the gospel truth.

It's the Saul Alinsky tactic of repetition to the nth degree, making the threat more terrifying than the thing itself. When they are proven wrong, none of these people in the MSM admit it but just go onto the next *Red Scare.*

Words are used to vilify any opposition, especially President Trump. The Alinsky tactic of *pick the target, freeze it, personalize it, and polarize it* has been the repeated theme of the MSM the past couple of years.

We are living in a time when those who are paying attention are horrified at the totalitarians and repressive regimentation of people's behaviors, so we become all robots to the Socialist/Marxist/Globalist nature of those at the top who want to control our lives.

From George Orwell's 1949 classic *1984, we now live in a time where true to Alinsky rule, "If you push a negative hard and deep enough, it will break through into its counter side; this is based on the principle that every positive has its negative."*

In part III Chapter 2 Deep State Figure, O'Brien is asking Winston Smith, a nonconformist, how many fingers he's holding up while Smith is being tortured to give into group thought. Finally, the pain becomes so unbearable Winston agrees that O'Brien is holding up 5 fingers when the reality is it's only 4.

Jonathan, as such, Barack Obama has met his match in Constitutional Karl. **Despite battered and beaten to a pulp, our friend Karl stood up to a Socialist whose only objective is to destroy all that we cherish to create *social justice and hope and change* as dictated by those in control.**

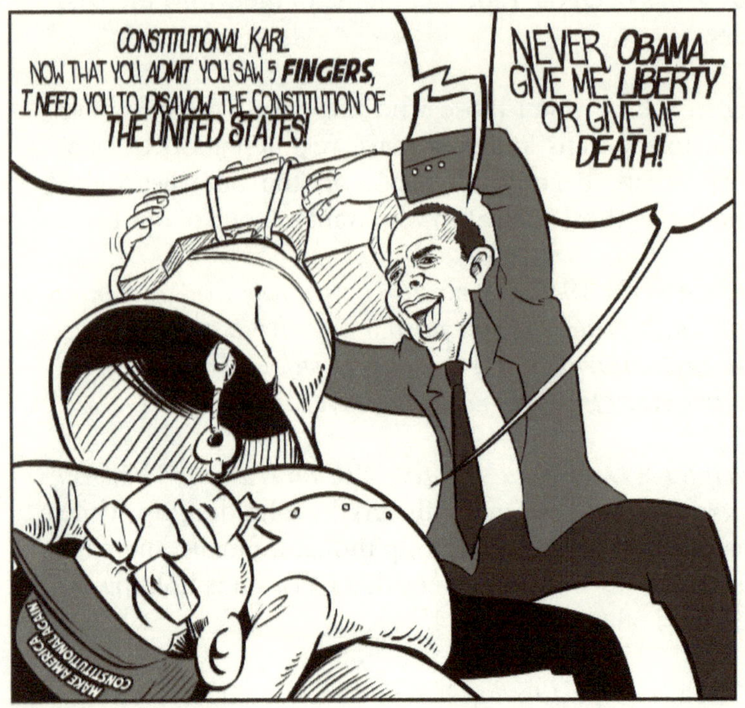

Note: No Constitutionalist was hurt when the illustrator was drawing this panel. As John Cameron Swayze once said, *"Constitutional Karl took a licking, but he's still ticking."*

In any event, the government is only as good as those who govern. When they abandon their constitutional duties to follow the law, all hell breaks loose. It doesn't matter which side of the political spectrum you are on, as those that fail to act to prevent these abuses only aide in further continuing the assault on our Constitution.

Lavrentiy Beria, the most ruthless and longest-serving secret police chief in Joseph Stalin's reign of terror in Russia and Eastern Europe, bragged that he could prove criminal conduct on anyone, even the innocent claiming, *"Show me the man, and I'll show you the crime."*

The difference between the Mueller investigation and the Kenneth Starr one in 1994 was there was never a crime to order a special counsel in the Trump-Russian probe. Clinton was charged by Kenneth Starr with lying under oath and obstruction of justice in the Paula Jones case. Eventually, going to the Senate for an impeachment vote, the Senate failed to give the 2/3 vote necessary for impeachment.

Bill Clinton eventually had his law license suspended as a result of the Monica Lewinsky scandal in 1996 and never filed to have it reinstated.

The Nixon special counsel had the Watergate break-in. Trump's only crime was winning the election and being able to expose those in the prior Administration who committed crimes.

Mueller was appointed by Rod Rosenstein, who Jeff Sessions appointed once he recused himself from the Russian investigation. Unlimited power was given by Rosenstein to Mueller to look for crimes and create ones from those who failed to remember or be consistent with their prior testimony. By the way, not that it's important, none of these inconsistencies had to do with Trump collusion with Russia to win the 2016 election.

Mueller went back in history to the Trump campaign associates and supporters to find crimes or create process crimes initiated from his investigation. Rosenstein was overseeing the investigation until President Trump finally fired Jeff Sessions and hired the new Attorney General, Bill Barr. Coincidently, Rosenstein then announced his retirement. But as the old saying goes, *"Justice delayed is justice denied."*

There are several deep state operatives who have had a statute of limitations expire on their crimes due to Jeff Sessions' failure to act. Now, unfortunately, as the system is broken, it's up to one man, the new Attorney General, Bill Barr, to see justice prevails.

It's a sad state that the system has failed to such an extent, that one man now decides whether those who sought to overthrow a legitimately elected President meet justice. A failure to prosecute will set the example that whenever we elect any President, social discord and violating individuals' constitutional rights by the opposition will become commonplace as there are no repercussions.

Hopefully, history will view Bill Barr as the *Superman of Liberty and Justice* for all. Barr must rise above the rhetoric and seek the truth, prosecuting those who violated the laws of the land despite the *kill the messenger* attitude of those who spew hatred of our Constitution and the rule of law being applied equally.

The question remains, as he was part of the establishment D.C. swamp for decades, is Barr going after the perpetrators and those who contributed to the real obstruction of high crimes, including his friend Robert Mueller?

There are many within the government who still refuse to do their jobs and are standing in the way of true justice by protecting those who have broken our laws. Why Christopher Wray, FBI Director at the time of this writing, is still defending lawbreakers by refusing to release documents pertaining to activities within the FBI, is as baffling as Sessions' refusal to do what was right and follow the rule of law.

Jonathan: *Dad, none of this makes common sense. Why was it permitted to continue unabated?*

Chapter 14

Doctrine of Common Sense

Jonathan, quite simply, the system failed as deep state bureaucrats and politicians took over our Constitution and determined those who oppose their rule of law will pay. It was my common sense that saw the reality from the fiction they created. It's not the *Common Sense* as outlined by Thomas Paine in his pamphlets from 1776-1777 that advocated independence from Great Britain, but the commonsense Ward and June Cleaver would impart on young Theodore (Beaver) Cleaver.

From a 1960 Episode from Leave it to Beaver entitled *Beaver and Kenneth,* here's the dialogue that would come back almost 60+ years later to spell out what really transpired with the Russians:

June Cleaver: *Well, Beaver, I just hope you realize that, wherever you go or whatever you do, there's always somebody watching you.*

Theodore 'Beaver' Cleaver: *Sure, mom. You watch me, and dad watches me, when I'm at school the teacher watches me, and when I go to the movies, the ushers watch me.*

June Cleaver: *No, Beaver, I mean somebody else.*

Theodore 'Beaver' Cleaver: Gee, *mom, do you mean like God?*

Then with the accuracy of Nostradamus, almost 60 years ago, a 12-year-old Theodore *Beaver* Cleaver would then say to his mother:

The Beav knew long ago that Russia was evil. Why on God's earth was something so perverse (The Mueller Special Counsel) permitted to happen to undermine our Great Republic? Putin's greatest misinformation advocates were those in our country, repeatedly spreading the Trump-Russia collusion narrative. His KGB couldn't have done a better job. What better way to dilute the power of the Presidency hiding your crimes than throwing out and perpetuating false stories as if they were true?

Jonathan: *Dad, you have Ward Cleaver reading The New York Times from December 17th, 1960 with the headline reading, Real Estate Mogul, Fred Trump's son, Donald, caught with ladies of the night at the Ritz Carlton in Moscow. The Ritz Carlton in Moscow didn't open until 2007?*

Jonathan, who cares? I'm taking a page from Jeff Zucker's, President of CNN Worldwide, proclamation that if I'm reporting what I believe is true, then it doesn't matter whether it is or not. Why waste 10 seconds of my life in finding out the truth, when the better story was to use a false narrative? Thank you, Mr. Zucker. You just need to change the advertisement for CNN to *"CNN the most Creative Name in Fake News."*

The truth is there was about as much chance of Donald Trump and his associates colluding with Russia to beat Hillary Clinton as there was with this big guy and his gang. When asked about the possibility that he and his posse were conspiring with Russia, this iconic figure said:

It wasn't the Russians who were the greatest threat to our Republic. It was those who thought to control and manipulate the outcome of an election to keep their power and control over us with all the treasures that come with that. Those who thought they were God, and we were their servants.

When the Russian interference with Trump campaign started, it didn't make any sense. How does someone who first ran for political office in June 2015 have the deep state connections needed for the collaboration to win an election? Plus, no Trump properties operate in Russia.

The Clintons have been in politics dating back to the 1970s. The Clinton Foundation has raised billions from foreign governments, including 145 million paid to the Clinton Foundation by Russian operatives. The narrative on Wikipedia spreads the myth about one individual contributing that amount—Frank Giustra, a Canadian businessman with Russian connections. But the money came from 8 Russian contributors through Canadian banks that made it impossible to track. Almost twenty percent of our uranium is now owned by Vladimir Putin. The Uranium One Scandal occurred when Hillary Clinton was Secretary of State under Obama, and Robert

Mueller was Director of the FBI. It required a sign off by CIFUS which included nine members including Secretaries of the Treasury, State (Clinton), Defense, Homeland Security, Commerce and Energy, Attorney General, and two White House Representatives with the President of the United States being the only one who could stop the deal.

Jonathan: *Was there any investigation of the deal?*

In close committee, there were some hearings. But to date, this real corrupt deal has not seen the light of day as former Obama Administration officials, Robert Mueller and Rod Rosenstein, two participants in its approval, have never been called to explain why such a deal went through with the Clintons benefitting in the long term. It's another example of big government doing things that the public should not know. The deep state and its MSM allies have diffused this bomb by deflecting and blaming low-level government officials on its approval. Again, it's how those in power in the government operate. The old saying, *"What's good for the goose, is good for the gander,"* does not apply.

It's truly a two-level system of justice where those in power, seen and unseen, can do anything to those they hate with no ramifications. It was one of the main reasons I voted for Donald Trump, to begin with. He owes no allegiance to anyone and was not firmly entrenched in the swamp of corruption that is Washington D.C. Truthfully, it's one of the main reasons Congress approval rating has been in the low teens for many years. People know most representatives are most likely to be in some rich person's pocket.

The details in this book are only to give you a reference point. To get to my conclusion, you must see the path I took to get there. That's why I provided the details to show you why things are so screwed up today, and we are in danger of a total collapse of all our constitutional rights.

The bureaucrats, whether they were Obama leftovers or individuals of both political parties, just couldn't stand Donald Trump as he was a disruptor of the status quo. Elected politicians, such as Adam

Schiff (D-CA), would purposely throw out lies as they realized there were no legal consequences. Per Art. I, Sec. 6 of the Constitution, which declares senators and representatives privileged from arrest during attendance at sessions and provides that *"for any speech or debate in either House, they shall not be questioned in any other place."* This guarantee had long been recognized as an essential right and was in line with the separation of powers and non-interference by the Executive and Judicial branches with the Legislature.

They came at Trump and his followers from all sides. When you have sitting Republican Senators in your own party like Jeff Flake and the late John McCain encouraging and lending credence into the narrative of Trump-Russian Collusion being responsible for winning the 2016 election, it's difficult to see the forest from the trees. The damage has been done, despite no proof of Trump or Trump campaign members and supporters interference from Russia. The stench of Washington D.C. runs deep, whether on the Democratic or Republican sides.

Key individuals within Mueller's investigation team had extreme hate toward Donald Trump, with two being excused due to damaging texts being discovered. It wasn't Robert Mueller who found the lovers Peter Strzok and Lisa Page texts. It was the Office of Inspector General. Yet, it took Mueller four months after the discovery to rid the two from the investigation. Prior to the election, these two, along with Bruce Ohr, DOJ criminal division officer, met with Christopher Steele, another major Trump hater, to see how to use his malicious Hillary Clinton funded document to get her elected President. Ohr's wife, Nellie, worked for Fusion GPS, who hired Christopher Steele to create the *dirty dossier.* Nellie also helped create some anti-Trump articles to spread in political circles.

Jonathan: *Dad, there's an old saying, "Oh, what a tangled web we weave when we first practice to deceive!" That's what's happening here?*

Jon, right on. When you deceive others to avert the truth, it eventually comes undone. Those who sought to subvert our Constitution were exposed only after Hillary Clinton did not win the election.

The corruption has been exposed only in media that care about the truth. But in the MSM world, if you don't cover it, it doesn't exist. Those involved in a Coup took the Hillary Clinton paid for and promoted *dirty trick dossier* and turned the tables on justice. At this point in time, most are skeptical of whether justice will ever be served.

Jonathan: *Dad, why are there no footnotes in this book?*

Jonathan, the Mueller Report goes to my point about footnotes being useless. In the report, there are tons of them. However, purposely, there is no drill down to the history as to why individuals singled out were even the subject of collusion, or what initiated the investigation of Trump and his associates.

In reading the Mueller report, there are countless footnotes linked to stories that propagated the Russian Hoax without exposing those who were a part of the effort to undermine Donald Trump's candidacy and then overthrow his Presidency. Footnotes are meaningless to the point that doesn't make true what the author is writing. I can make anyone believe anything by cross-referencing sources that were untrue from the get-go. That's why there are no footnotes in this book.

Due to my attention to detail and audit background, I could write a book alone on the back story as to what was purposely omitted from the Mueller Report. As such, the over $32 million spent on an over 2½-year investigation into something that didn't happen was nothing more than obstruction from prosecuting those who perpetuated a myth and colluded in trying to overthrow a duly elected President.

Bottom line, it's up to each and everyone in this country to sort through all the information out there and arrive at their own conclusions. Jonathan, the truth is easier to find than those who want to control our thoughts want you to believe. It starts with common sense. And that is the foundation of this book. Ronald Reagan once said, *"Trust but verify."* Today, it's *don't trust but verify.*

Though to validate many of my claims, at the back of the book, I will give credit to those publications and individuals who shaped my beliefs. Consensus does not always equal reality. But common sense should be the foundation of any belief and not emotion. This book ties everything I've learned from others into one coherent story that has as its basis common sense.

There's a common thread against those who have written books supporting the Trump-Russia conspiracy theory. They use the phony Christopher Dossier to support their claims. There's a common thread among those who have written books showing corruption from within and no conspiracy with Russia. Tons of footnotes and cross-references that go between books.

Chapter 15

Destroying the Lives of Those Who Served

And like the persecution of Paul Robeson during the 1950s' *Red Scare*, the Obama Administration and Robert Mueller special counsel targeted retired Lieutenant General Michael Flynn, a 33 year veteran of the military. The planned destruction of General Flynn's life started when he was in the Obama Administration. Flynn briefly served as National Security Advisor for President Trump. He was the victim of one of the over 300 illegal un-masking in 2016 and surveillance tapes by the Obama Administration through Deputy Attorney General, Sally Yates, National Security Advisor Susan Rice, and the United States Ambassador to the UN, Samantha Powers. While serving as Director of Defense Intelligence Agency **during the Obama Administration, Flynn was viewed as a threat** *"to the military-industrial complex."* This phrase was coined by President Dwight D. Eisenhower during his farewell speech on January 17th, 1961.

As Senator Chuck Schumer (D-NY), on January 3rd, 2017, said, *"Let me tell you: You take on the intelligence community—they have six ways from Sunday at getting back at you."* Although he meant it about Donald Trump, it was directed more to Lt. General Michael Flynn. President Trump has fought back as he holds the largest pulpit in the world. Lt. General Flynn was going one on one with the deep state that saw him as an outlier in the Obama Administration. After Trump's election and Flynn being placed as Trump's National Security Advisor, the deep state went ballistic against him as now he was a real threat to the Socialist/Globalist policies President Obama had put in place.

When Flynn was Director of the Defense Intelligence Agency (July 2012–August 2014), he was in repeated conflicts with Obama's policies on ISIS and Iran. Eventually forced out, he remained a critic of their policies. When appointed by President Trump as his National Security Advisor, Flynn was set up by the FBI Director James Comey, former FBI Assistant Director, Andrew McCabe, and former FBI Chief of the Counterespionage Section, Peter Strzok in a meeting without legal representation. This meeting is brilliantly documented in Greg Jarrett's book, *The Russia Hoax: The Illicit Scheme to Clear Hillary Clinton and Frame Donald Trump (pages 191-209)*. The details are stunning, starting with what Sally Yates, Deputy Attorney General, did to use the full weight and financial resources of the U.S. government against a 33-year military man, Lt. Colonel Michael Flynn, because of the perceived threat he was to Obama and his Administration's policies. In addition, Yates was one of the four signers on the illegal FISA warrant using the fictitious Steele Dossier to surveil Carter Page.

At the time of this writing, Sydney Powell was retained by the Lt. Colonel as his legal counsel. This legal stalwart knows all too well the prosecutorial abuses of Weissmann and Mueller. Not a good day for either to be sure.

In 2015, the Obama Administration and its surrogates unmasked 3 individuals. In 2016, the unmaskings were an incredible 306. When an individual is unmasked, **unmasking** is the term being used in the press about decisions to uncover people who were incidentally caught up in routine surveillance of foreign officials.

In any event, when first interviewed by the FBI's Andrew McCabe, former Assistant FBI Director, and Peter Strzok, former Chief of Counterespionage and head investigator in the Clinton email server, they found Flynn to be truthful. Then a few months after Mueller was appointed head of the Russia-Trump investigation in December 2017, a once truthful Flynn was found to be making false statements. Mueller and his team put the screws to Flynn, where he eventually pleaded guilty to making false statements about a meeting with a Russian ambassador. Additionally, Mueller and his gangs of hooligans threatened Flynn by saying they will go after his son if he doesn't cop a plea. Although illegal acts were committed by the Obama Administration and the FBI in setting Flynn up, it's Lt. General Flynn who ends up bankrupt and losing his home.

True and equal justice was not what the deep state through Robert Muller's Special Counsel was looking for. If so, Joseph Mifsud, a Maltese scholar and paid government informant, on three occasions was caught lying to the FBI in the Mueller report, and yet, no charges were brought against him.

Jonathan: *Dad, for being an old man, your memory and attention to detail is incredible.*

Thank you, Jonathan. I think stories that are made up and repeated numerous times by the mainstream media become fact only because of being ingrained in any anti-Trump story. It's a Saul Alinsky tactic of repeating something to no end makes it a fact despite lack of evidence and only the emotion to support that allegation. Typically, no one in the MSM questions the legitimacy of the story, as they like the narrative.

The lawbreakers who came out with this collusion scam were never the focus of the MSM. It starts at the top, working its way down to Loretta Lynch, James Comey, Andrew McCabe, Peter Strzok and Lisa Page, FBI attorney James Baker, CIA Director Brennan, National Intelligence Director Clapper, and a whole slew of paid foreign intelligence assets. Why come clear on an investigation that never should have been started if your main goal is to have Hillary Clinton elected President? Then after that failed, to impeach or destroy a sitting President instead of tainting the suspect legacy of Barack Obama?

Jonathan, the detail and depth of corruption within the Obama Administration is stunning. And with each passing day, as more becomes known, the level of criminality within our government has never been seen in this country's history. **President Trump, on March 2nd, 2019 at the CPAC (Conservative Political Action Conference), summed up the Mueller investigation as a witch hunt that is *"trying to get me out with bullshit."* This has been Trump's repeated theme since the investigation started.**

The book Mueller is referencing is the New York Times Bestseller, *Witch Hunt, Strategies from the Salem Witch Trials of 1692 to Incorporate in a Coup d'etat.*

What makes common sense is to call in the source of the leaks, Julian Assange, to testify before a full Congressional Committee. Assange should be granted immunity to testify.

In an interview with **Sean Hannity**, on January 4th, 2017, he was asked by Hannity, *"So in other words, let me be clear...Russia did not give you the Podesta documents or anything from the DNC?"*

The Australian founder of the whistleblowing website, who has been living in the Ecuadorian embassy in London until recently, responded: *"That's correct."*

Assange further stated: *"We're unhappy that we felt that we needed to even say that it wasn't a state party. Normally, we say nothing at*

*all. We have ... a strong interest in protecting our sources, and so
we never say anything about them, never ruling anyone in or anyone
out. And so here, in order to prevent a distraction attack against our
publications, we've had to come out and say no, it's not a state party.*
***Stop trying to distract in that way and pay attention to the content of
the publication.***"

Jonathan, to this day, there has been no definitive proof that
Assange was lying. His reputation is built on honesty, as all publications in WikiLeaks go through a thorough vetting process. It's very
suspicious that the Mueller Report comes out after Assange is arrested and totally silenced.

Assange also revealed that WikiLeaks received *"about three pages
of information to do with the [Republican National Committee] and
Donald Trump [during the campaign], but it was already public
somewhere else."* The primary reason is that Donald Trump does
not use email.

Then on April 11th, 2019, Assange was arrested by the U.K. police
being taken forcibly from the Ecuadorian Embassy in London. The
U.K. detained Assange with the U.S. charges involving conspiring
to hack a Pentagon network in 2010 to obtain documentation using
Bradley Manning, former U.S. Army intelligence officer. The information published by WikiLeaks showed atrocities committed by
the U.S. troops against Iraqi citizens, more civilians had been killed
than government officials estimated, and other documentation
showing our military atrocities. These documents later became
known as *"the Iraqi War Logs"* and *"Afghan War Diary."* Manning
was arrested again on March 8th, 2019, as she is being held in custody
due to her refusal to testify in front of a grand jury about WikiLeaks.
She's in a Northern Virginia jail at the time of this writing.

The U.S. currently has an outstanding warrant based on 17 indict-
ments against Assange, including espionage demanding extradition
to the United States for publishing secret documents on WikiLeaks.
A hearing is scheduled in the U.K. for extradition in February 2020.
As outlined prior, Mike Pompeo, Secretary of State, views
Assange's acts as espionage. The case our government has against

Assange is very weak at best. Referring to Daniel Ellsberg and the *Pentagon Papers*, a conviction seems unlikely (although again, I'm no lawyer).

In any event, Assange's arrest was significant in that the Russian conspirators, the freedom of speech advocates, and deep state forces tied to the *military-industrial complex* came out either praising or condemning the arrest. Due to my Asperger's Syndrome, as outlined in my second book, *Dad, Why Are You So Weird?*, my focus is limited and usually pretty accurate as I try not to let outside distractions affect what really matters to me. As President Trump is tied close to the military as witnessed by substantial budget appropriations since he came into office and his allegiance and love of our armed forces, it's difficult to see whether he can separate himself from how the military intelligentsia view Assange (guilty of the high crimes).

Although he is not a citizen of the United States, many are outraged about Julian Assange's arrest based on his freedom of speech rights being violated. Assange is one of the rare legitimate journalists who has never been proven wrong in any of his WikiLeaks publications.

Another irony of his arrest was how the MSM continued to feed into the collusion of Assange and Russia to conspire with Trump people to ensure Trump became President. It has always been commonsense in my mind that Assange is granted immunity from prosecution by testifying before Congress as to where he obtained the DNC information and the Podesta emails.

Based on how President Trump factors in both sides of the argument prior to making any decision, his gut instinct based on knowledge is to always lean toward his conviction. In other words, until Julian Assange is on United States soil, do not presuppose anything as to how he is going to be treated (i.e., friend or foe).

Jonathan: *Dad, if President Trump doesn't grant Julian Assange immunity, much like after World War II, we granted Wernher von Braun, would you think any less of him?*

Most certainly. It's always been apparent to me that the Deep State operatives exposed in this book and many others, do not want Assange testifying anywhere. Without Assange's eye-witness account, many more books will be written in the ensuing decades detailing how Trump colluded with Russia to win the 2016 election. What Assange represents to Constitutionalists is our 1ˢᵗ Amendment rights. It's a right many governments around the world will never recognize. I hope the President acknowledges history and how the truth always matters, and with that, the commonsense of having the one accused of high crimes provide proof as to what transpired.

If this does come to fruition, it will be a ***must-watch TV event.*** Having been glued to the television during the Watergate Hearings in 1974, with Julian Assange front and center, all viewing records around the world would be broken...and with that, the back of the deep state operatives who brought us on the verge of a constitutional crisis. Assange, as polarizing as he is, will bring viewership of those who never sought the truth (the Closed Minders), along with those lost in their world of social media, the Oblivions, who for one moment in time will put down their cell phones and pay attention to what almost happened in our country.

Until Julian Assange can come forward, many in this country will view the Trump-Russian collusion/obstruction narrative based on party affiliation and/or hatred for Donald Trump no matter what comes out of the Barr investigations and criminal charges that follow. Assange goes beyond party affiliation as it will be nearly impossible to refute what he has to say.

Chapter 16

Anatomy of High Crimes and Treason – Part 1

The table is now set. April 1st, 2020: Julian Assange is set to testify before a House Intelligence Committee headed by Congressman, Adam Schiff (D-CA).

In addition, each first-day witness, other than Assange, is injected with truth serum due to their propensity to lie. Although causing a great stir among Democrats, mainstream Republican establishment, and deep state players, the President under Executive Order ruled this is mandatory as the truth can never be compromised.

The narrative below is just my imagination and, although real in my mind, it's still my vision as to what transpired. For relevancy purposes, I've eliminated questions that have no bearing on the truth, other than Adam Schiff's. Schiff's support in being elected to office came from Moveon.org and George Soros. As such, Schiff is not his own man.

Adam Schiff: *Mr. Assange, we appreciate you coming here and testifying before our committee. Before we start, I would like to give our accepted view of what has transpired to give Trump the Presidency of the United States. Quite simply, we all accepted collusion with Russia was the reason. You are here to verify this conclusion. As such, I'm just asking for a **yes** or **no** response. First question, Mr. Assange, have you ever had Russian caviar?*

Julian Assange: *Yes.*

Schiff: *Mr. Assange, have you ever drank Russian Vodka?*

Assange: *Yes.*

Schiff: *Last of my food and beverage questions. Mr. Assange, have you ever had borscht?*

Assange looks up in amazement, shaking his head in disbelief.

Jerold Nadler bursts in, stating, "*Mr. Assange, we need to get these answers to get at the root of Trump-Russian interference in our elections.*"

Assange: *Yes.*

Schiff: *Finally, Mr. Assange, have you ever heard the name Roger Stone, who was a Trump supporter?*

Assange: *Yes.*

Schiff: *I rest my case. I've just proved Russian Interference in the election to get Trump elected President.*

Devin Nunes: *Chairman Schiff, you are supported by dark money from your Puppet Master George Soros that has infiltrated the House of Representatives and Senate with individuals and groups on both sides of the political spectrum that hate our Constitution and the rule of law.*

Over three years into a fake investigation, and you still have no proof of collusion, as you claim. The over $32 million that was wasted on investigations that continue to look into a crime that never happened should be taken out of the Congressional salaries and wealth of members who supported this witch hunt along with the perpetrators in the Obama Administration, Justice Department, FBI, CIA, and the MSM who have gone to destroy the very fabric of what our Constitution guarantees in the Bill of Rights.

Chairman Schiff, either you're a political operative calling for the destruction of our country, or you don't know if...

Nunes goes on to say, *"the Republicans on our committee have agreed to turn all questions and time over to the defender of truth and justice, Perry Mason."*

Perry Mason: *Now, Mr. Assange, whether people believe in your right to publish information in WikiLeaks, you have always been truthful, and there is no one out there who has been able to disprove what you've published as false. Also, there has been no definitive proof contrary to your claim that WikiLeaks information was not obtained from Russia or Russian affiliates. Thank you for being here. My first question centers around the sources of the DNC and Podesta leaks. Can you verify under oath that neither a Russian nor Russian state operative provided you with the information you published on WikiLeaks?*

Assange*: Mr. Mason, that is correct.*

Mason: *Mr. Assange, can you specifically state the source of both the DNC and Podesta emails?*

Assange: *The source of the DNC emails worked inside the DNC. Due to concerns for the family, I will show you this information in closed committee. It's the actual thumb drive this source provided.*

Mason: *Was there any reason why WikiLeaks announced a $20,000 reward for information on DNC insider, Seth Rich, who was murdered on July 10th, days before the DNC email leaks on July 22nd, 2016?*

Assange: *Mr. Mason, I can only say our source will be revealed in closed committee. The family has concerns for their safety should the name be released. It goes to the underbelly of the deep state operations in the United States.*

Mason: *Has there been any other incident in WikiLeaks history where you announced a reward for someone killed as you did when you offered $20,000 for information on Rich's murder?*

Assange: *No.*

Mason: *Mr. Assange, do you not find it strange that the DNC did not offer a reward for his murder while WikiLeaks did?*

Assange: *Mr. Mason, you would have to ask them why they didn't. It would be only speculation on my part as to why. But in their defense after the murder, they did name a bicycle rack outside the DNC in his honor.*

Mason: *Did Robert Mueller ever contact you?*

Assange: *No. I was very willing to give evidence to Mueller via video link while I was holed up in the Ecuadorian embassy in London. Mr. Mueller was aware of this. Obviously, because it would destroy the narrative he and his so-called investigators built up, why would they want to interview me?*

Mason: *I recommend an adjournment so we can review Mr. Assange's source for the DNC hacks.*

Schiff: *I don't see the point, but to pacify those who still believe President Trump didn't collude with Russia, we will adjourn briefly.*

Upon returning:

Schiff: *After reviewing the original source for the DNC leaks, I have concluded although it was not Russia who provided the thumb drive, the individual who provided the information had to have Russian ties. I will order a thorough investigation into the ties of the leaker. Although, this might be extremely difficult as he is no longer with us.*

Mason: *Mr. Assange, can you now provide us the source of the Podesta emails?*

Assange: *Mr. Podesta is not very smart as his password to access his emails was "password." Multiple individuals and groups hacked his Gmail account. Again, due to security concerns for those who provide information, I will provide the original source documents in closed session.*

Mason: *Again, I wish adjournment to review source information.*

Schiff: *I don't see the point as to whatever the source is, it's all tied to Russia. But I will pacify you again.*

Upon returning:

Schiff: *Well again, although the source is not Russia, they had to be behind it as this information will destroy the Trump-Russia collusion delusion. I will have another special committee convene to find Russian ties into the leaker.*

Nunes: *Wow! Chairman Schiff, your stupidity is only exceeded by your corruption. We should order a special committee in order to examine your sanity. Mr. Mason, please continue.*

Mason: *What did the Podesta emails reveal?*

Assange: *It revealed potential pay-or-play while Hillary Clinton was Secretary of State; how the DNC derailed Bernie Sanders and his campaign; the power structure in this country and how corrupt it is; John Podesta, Clinton's lead campaign advisor, writing Clinton has* *terrible instincts; that President Obama was aware of Hillary's private server; that Hillary was fed a question by Donna Brazile in a CNN DNC debate; disclosed Hillary's two different personas for the public and in private to large donors; collusion with the DOJ to subvert damaging information on Hillary and, the disgust Clinton has for religious individuals and minorities among other things.*

Mason: Mr. Assange, what did the DNC emails reveal?

Assange: It revealed that the DNC was subverting Bernie Sanders's campaign with Debbie Wasserman Schultz, DNC Chairwoman, a major part of the sabotage. She later had to resign as a result. It also confirmed a lot that was in the John Podesta emails.

Mason: I guess then that nothing very damaging came out of exposing Hillary Clinton and her cronies for what they did?

Mason: Final question. Mr. Assange, has anything that WikiLeaks published been disproved?

Assange: No. In fact, ever since we started publishing WikiLeaks in 2006, nothing has been disproved. We used the process of vetting the information to ensure its reliability. It's a lost art in American journalism.

Mason: *At this point, as much has been revealed and verified, the tension in this room is at an extremely high level. We all need to relax and to relieve our stress by exercising. I call on fitness guru, Jack LaLanne, with his dog, Walter, to lead us in a short session.*

The Committee was adjourned with the next witness to be Robert Mueller.

Chapter 17

Anatomy of High Crimes and Treason – Part II – The Perpetrators

Later that day, on April 1ˢᵗ, 2020, the Schiff Committee reassembles. Robert Mueller is the next witness.

Schiff: *Mr. Mueller, I know you are here against your will. Can you tell us what transpired to get you here?*

Robert Mueller: *There was a pre-dawn raid on March 31ˢᵗ with 29 FBI agents, attack dogs, and 13 FBI vehicles along with helicopters hovering in front of my personal residence. My wife and I, along with our dogs, were terrified. The agents put me in handcuffs and read me my Miranda rights. One agent told me I was charged with over 100 felonies going back decades with the recent charge,*

including ordering the destruction of the cell phones of FBI lovers, Peter Strzok and Lisa Page.

It was Strzok and Page that played a significant role in both the Clinton and Trump investigations. They hated Donald Trump so much so the information on their cells had to be destroyed as both were originally on my counsel to investigate Trump-Russia collusion. Furthermore, each had already been a part of an FBI investigation into Russia-Trump collusion 90 days prior to Rosenstein appointing me to head the Witch Hunt into collusion. BTW, after the 90 days, they found no collusion.

Schiff: *Mr. Mueller, I'm sorry for the way you were treated because you were only trying to bring down a bigoted, racist, homophobe, corrupt, unpresidential, and all things bad President. If ever there was a crime you committed, then I'm in George Soros's pockets. It's just terrible that other than those who support President Trump, others lose their constitutional rights in bringing down this insane man.*

Schiff: *I'm done with my questioning and turn it over to Perry Mason.*

Mason: **Mr. Mueller, nice teddy bear? Where did you get it?**

Mueller: **Roger Stone lent it to me.**

Mason: *Now for the tough questions. Mr. Mueller, you were injected with truth serum against your wishes, is that correct?*

Mueller: *Correct. Why would I want to tell the truth now after over three years of finding nothing against President Trump in colluding with the Russians to win the election? Especially because, like Sargent Schultz of Hogan Heroes, "I know nothing" as I was only a figurehead giving Andrew Weissmann cover to prosecute and make up crimes against Donald Trump and his cronies. It was a nice paycheck, too.*

Mason: *Mr. Mueller, why did you agree to head the Special Coun-sel's investigation into Donald Trump?*

Mueller: *Mr. Mason, I've always been a deep state player, and alt-hough no longer at the top of my prosecutorial game, I delegated complete authority to Andrew and his team of pit bulls. He has a reputation of knowing how to skirt the law and apply pressure to anyone who goes against the establishment and deeply entrenched bureaucrats maintaining the status quo. The status quo is what gives us our power over the country, and with that, financial prosperity and control over the common man.*

Also, I knew there were bigger problems for the prior Administra-tion, including the DOJ, FBI, and CIA and any other 3-letter organ-ization as crimes were committed that none of us felt would have ever been exposed had Hillary Clinton been elected President. In addition, we had the support of the establishment Republican party and/or the Never Trumpers, the MSM, and the help of the radical left-wing of the Democratic party. People became so delusional that everything Trump has at its basis some form of hate that made it easier to get away with throwing away Trump and his supporters' constitutional rights.

Mason: *So basically Mr. Mueller, President Trump was viewed as a disrupter, and that's not to be tolerated by those who control the levers of power, especially if it means bringing down those who you were in cahoots with the past couple of decades?*

Mueller: *Correct. As I was a very little part of the investigation, leav-ing prosecutorial discretion to Andrew Weissmann to use the full force and backing of the United States government to destroy inno-cent people's lives, I have no idea as to what transpired. Plus, many of the Weissmann appointees were a part of the Obama Admin-istration's DOJ who were involved in preventing Trump from be-coming President and the coup afterward. These same individuals then colluded and obstructed to prevent prosecution for crimes they committed by throwing a shadow over Trump and his associates. We, deep state players, are proud of our achievements, including standing in the way of Trump releasing all information pertaining to the Kennedy Assassination.*

Mason: *Mr. Mueller, who were your targets in the Trump-Russia collusion investigation?*

Mueller: *Anyone who was a public person who supported Donald Trump for Presidency and mentioned in the Steele Dossier. We would pursue them to no end, hoping they "will sing and compose." Then afterward, we looked for individuals who supported Trump and who are known as flame throwers, as this made it easy for the prosecutors to catch them in conflicting testimony. They needed to be taught a lesson that anyone who supports someone who isn't an establishment choice on either side needs to be destroyed. After all, Weissmann had the resources of the United States government behind him. No one can match his prosecutorial powers. I'm proud of the fact that Weissmann had the power to destroy people's lives, as we've shown over the decades. I had no problem in him using it, along with others appointed to the Special Counsel. These individuals had a track record of prosecutorial abuse bringing injustice to people they hated.*

Mason: *Mr. Mueller, to reiterate your prior comments, are you saying that you did not play an active part in the investigation?*

Mueller: *Other than depositing my checks and signing off on the report with my name and hiring Weissmann as my attack dog, I was busy doing other more important things? On a few occasions, I met with Andrew and canceled several golf dates with friends.*

Mason: *Mr. Mueller, you went after Paul Manafort for tax crimes, money laundering, and foreign filing violations. You granted immunity to Tony Podesta, brother to Hillary Clinton's former campaign manager, John Podesta, to testify against Manafort. It appears that Tony, through his entity the Podesta Group, was in cahoots with Manafort on a number of these crimes committed with Ukraine. Is that true?*

Mueller: *That's true. Weissmann told me that Podesta was even more guilty than Manafort as the Podesta Group collected millions over the years through fraudulent behaviors. Why do you think Tony Podesta stepped down as CEO of Podesta Group prior to his immunity deal? He thought he was going to go down, too.*

Mason: *Then why did you not grant immunity to Manafort and persecute Podesta?*

Mueller: *Mr. Mason, I went after no one. However, Weissmann told me that going after Podesta would dilute the narrative of how evil Trump and his associates are. After all, the Podestas have been in the Clinton pockets, like many of us, for decades. Mr. Mason, when is this truth serum going to wear off?*

Mason: *Mr. Mueller, almost done with you. Thank you for finally telling the truth. It's only that you had no choice this time. Now, to the Steele Dossier. Did you ever investigate the individual Christopher Steele who created it, and who would never verify any part of it? Or investigate the funders of the dossier, including Hillary Clinton, Fusion GPS, and a Russian oligarch?*

Mueller: *Frankly, I know nothing about any of what you asked me. However, Andrew told me there would be no point in going after the truth as it would destroy the narrative of Trump-Russia collusion he and his team were trying to create. Weissmann explained he and his team of deep state bureaucrats needed to deflect away from the crimes they committed by creating crimes against Trump associates and trying to find anything that President Trump could be prosecuted on.*

Mason: *Mr. Mueller, tell us about your involvement in the Uranium One Scandal where the Clinton Foundation was given $145 million after 8 Russians eventually gave Vladimir Putin control of 20 percent of the uranium in our country? Also, William Campbell, an FBI informant, provided you information about the corruption involving the Clintons and Rosatom, the Russian controlled Nuclear agency, prior to you permitting this deal to go through. Why was that?*

The truth serum wears off with Robert Mueller in a state of shock, stating, "*Mr. Mason, you have violated my Constitutional Rights and my ability to declare the 5th Amendment by drugging me and forcing me to testify. I had the right to plead the 5th. This is an Aobamnation!*"

Mason: *Not as bad as you and your hoodlums using the full force of the United States government against individuals whose only crime was to support Donald Trump. The crimes you convicted Manafort and Cohen of should have been brought by district courts years ago. You only charged them now as you couldn't find any Trump-Russia collusion. It was always a collusion delusion.*

Mueller: *Mr. Mason, the truth serum wore off, so I plead the 5th. Also, I need to go peepee.*

Schiff: *We need to take another recess as I hate people, Mr. Mason, who seek the truth! You're excused, Mr. Mueller, and a word of advice. Get legal counsel.*

Session reconvenes with the next witness James Comey.

Schiff: *Mr. Comey, I know you are here against your will. Can you tell us what transpired to get you here?*

James Comey: *There was a pre-dawn raid on March 31ˢᵗ with 29 FBI agents, attack dogs, and 13 FBI vehicles along with helicopters hovering in front of my personal residence. My wife and I, along with our dogs, were terrified. The agents put me in handcuffs and read me my Miranda rights and told of crimes I committed that would take over two hours to explain.*

Schiff: *Mr. Comey, I'm sorry for the way you were treated because you were only trying to bring down a bigoted, racist, homophobe, unpresidential, corrupt, and all things bad President. If ever there was a crime you committed, then I'm in George Soros' sockets. It's just terrible that other than those who support President Trump, others lose their constitutional rights in bringing down this insane man. Mr. Mason, proceed.*

Mason: *Former Director Comey, why did you come out on July 5ᵗʰ, 2016, and exonerate Hillary Clinton?*

Comey: *When Attorney General Loretta Lynch met with Bill Clinton on the infamous Tarmac meeting on June 15th, 2016, the word was Former President Clinton told Lynch if she gets the government off Hillary's back in the email investigation, a Supreme Court nomination awaits. What was I supposed to do? She had tied our hands on all investigations into the Clinton email server, even restricting access to emails that pertained to the Clinton Foundation. An arrangement was made between Lynch and Clinton's attorneys to exonerate her in this "matter." By the way, one of the Foundation's attorneys was Jeannie Rhee, who was appointed by my friend, Robert Mueller, to serve on the Trump-Russia Collusion Investigation. It's like the fox guarding the henhouse. How corrupt is that?*

Mason: *Mr. Comey, we appreciate your honesty. But, again, without the truth serum, you would give us nothing but double talk. **Mr. Comey, do you believe President Obama was aware of everything that was going on in the Clinton email server investigation and the phony investigation into Trump-Russia collusion?***

Comey: *Yes. It came from the very top that Hillary was not going to be indicted, and Trump implicated in a Russian Scandal. We granted immunity to testify to many members of the Clinton campaign team, unlike limited immunity granted to Trump associates if they spilled the beans or created their own beanstalk of Trump crimes.*

In addition, Barack Obama issued an executive order prior to leaving the office on January 12th, 2017. This order gave the NSA permission to disseminate raw signals intelligence information among 16 intelligence gathering governmental agencies. New Executive order 12333 was enacted as President Obama knew that many of his Administrative personnel, including Obama National Security Advisor, Susan Rice, Acting Attorney General, Sally Yates, and U.S. Ambassador, Samantha Powers, unmasked over 300 Trump associates to find political dirt on his campaign to be used by Clinton and her associates. Then shockingly, when Clinton lost, a phony Mueller Investigation started to divert attention away from the real criminals.

Mason: *Mr. Comey, your memos that were leaked to the press of your discussions with President Trump by your professor friend, who later became your attorney, are the documents that contributed to Rod Rosenstein starting the Mueller Russia Investigation. You also signed a FISA warrant using the Steele Dossier that you told the President was full of, as you put it, "salacious and unverified information." Just from a commonsense point of view, isn't it a crime to submit unverified information to the FISA court to get an order to surveil Trump campaign members?*

Comey: *Obviously, it is. But our people and the individuals at the top of the Obama Administration play by our own rules. We were desperate to distract from our misdeeds with a phony investigation. Lovers, Peter Strzok and Lisa Page, testified that they gave notes on both scandals to me to brief President Obama.*

Mason: **Mr. Comey, a lot of what you said in your prior testimony and public exoneration of Hillary Clinton made no sense. Can you tell us why she had a server in her bathroom in Chappaqua, New York?**

Comey: **Obviously, as Secretary of State, she was giving favors to those who made donations to the Clinton Foundation and its off-shoot, the Clinton Global Initiative.** *The foundation has long been accused of 'pay-to-play' transactions.*

As reported in International Business Times: "The Clinton-led State Department authorized $151 billion in Pentagon-brokered deals to 16 countries that donated to the Clinton Foundation—a 145 percent increase in completed sales to those nations over the same time frame during the Bush Administration." The fact I said she was not guilty of a crime, and only extremely careless, just shows how far I had to go to exonerate her and take the heat off Loretta Lynch. Pure logic showed that Hillary Clinton was as guilty as sin. The fact the FBI was banned from viewing pertinent emails into her crimes by the DOJ was not revealed until much later. I did my best to cover up the collusion scandal within the Obama Administration.

Mason: *Mr. Comey, what was the underlying reason you and your associates acted the way they did?*

Comey: *It's like Chick Hearn, famous Lakers announcer, once said, "the mustard fell off the hot dog" as no one thought Donald Trump would be elected President. Everyone involved had to hide crimes they committed that would never be discovered when Hillary became President. But that didn't happen, and now, we've been exposed for the criminals we are. Some would call this a* **silent coup d'état.**

Mason: *John Solomon wrote in The Hill on July 16ᵗʰ, 2019, on the FBI spreadsheet kept on the Steele Dossier; I quote: "Multiple sources familiar with the FBI spreadsheet tell me most Steele's claims were deemed to be wrong or could not be corroborated even with the most awesome tools available to the U.S. intelligence community. One source estimated the spreadsheet found upward of 90 percent of the dossier's claims to be either wrong, unverifiable, or open-source intelligence found with a Google search."*

Further on, John Solomon said that based on the FBI spreadsheet, you told President Trump that the Dossier was "salacious and unverified." But Mr. Comey, is it true that despite knowing the Trump-Russia investigation had no basis, you kept it going?

Comey: *Mr. Mason, I had no choice. Either we kept it going or face true justice and spend our remaining days on Alcatraz Island.*

Mason: Finally, Mr. Comey, were you not the one who nixed the idea of having Julian Assange come to the States under an immunity agreement. This was a deal arranged by former DOJ 4ᵗʰ in command Bruce Ohr, Senator Mark Warner (D-VA) and democratic attorney who was negotiating for Assange. In exchange for immunity, Mr. Assange would provide technical evidence and discussion regarding who did not engage in the DNC releases and Podesta hacks and help address flaws in the security systems that led to the loss of the U.S. cyber weapons program. If you were the one, please tell us why.

Comey: *I was the one who told Ohr to stand down. The reason was simple. If I'm trying to cover the tracks of my crimes and those of my associates, why would I want to have the truth come out that destroys the Russian-Trump collusion narrative? I sincerely felt Donald Trump is not mentally fit to serve as President, and as such, the Alinsky rule that a particular false means justifies a self-righteous end.*

Mason: *Mr. Comey, you are excused.*

Schiff: *Mr. Comey, like I said for Robert Mueller, it's time to lawyer up.*

A recess is called with the next witness to be Rod Rosenstein.

Schiff: *Mr. Rosenstein, I know you are here against your will. I can't go on with any questioning as I'm afraid my supporters (i.e., deep state) will be upset at me if I ask any questions that reveal the truth. But what happened to make sure you are here is a violation of your constitutional rights as you constantly avoided appearances before Congress. Can you describe what transpired?*

Rod Rosenstein: *There was a pre-dawn raid on March 31ˢᵗ with 29 FBI agents and attack dogs and 13 FBI vehicles in front of my personal residence. My wife and I, along with our dogs, were terrified. One agent read me my Miranda rights and said I was charged with signing a false FISA warrant based on a salacious dossier that was never verified. Further, my crimes included being a part of an attempted overthrow of a duly-elected President initiating a phony investigation into no crime.*

Schiff: *Mr. Rosenstein, I'm sorry for the way you were treated because you were only trying to bring down a bigoted, racist, homophobe, unpresidential, corrupt, and all things bad President. If there ever was a crime you committed, then I'm in George Soros's pockets. It's just terrible that people other than those who support President Trump lose their constitutional rights in bringing down this insane man.*

No further questions, Mr. Rosenstein. I need to get a drink. My deep state backers are furious that constitutional rights apply to those who oppose our views. The 2-tier system of justice needs to prevail if I'm to remain in power.

Mason: *Mr. Rosenstein, why did you order a special counsel into the investigation of Donald Trump brought about by the Comey letters and the letter you wrote firing James Comey as FBI Director?*

Rosenstein: *I signed one of the four warrants using the fake unverified dossier. I needed to deflect from real crimes I committed along with my friends, who are also deep state operatives.*

Mason: **You appointed Robert Mueller as special counsel based on 28 CFR §600.1 Grounds for appointing a Special Counsel that states, "The Attorney General, or in cases in which the Attorney General is recused, the Acting Attorney General, will appoint a Special Counsel when he or she determines that criminal investigation of a person or matter is warranted."**

Former Assistant Attorney General Rosenstein, what specifically warranted a criminal investigation into President Trump?

Rosenstein: *He won the Presidency.*

Mason: *Thank you for your honesty. But again, you had no choice as you've been injected with truth serum. So, basically, as conflicted as you were, you needed to divert attention from crimes you and others committed in the prior Administration. This diversion was not because you ever felt President Trump and his associates committed crimes, but you and your cohorts were caught red-handed when Clinton did not win?*

Rosenstein: *That's correct. With the assistance of the MSM and others on both sides of the political spectrum who hated this President, it wasn't such a big leap to think we could get away with it.*

Mason: *Mr. Rosenstein, part of your responsibility after Jeff Sessions, the then acting Attorney General recused himself, was to oversee Mueller and his team to ensure they were following the law and your order on the scope of Russian collusion. How did you do that?*

Rosenstein: *Truthfully, I spent most of my time playing golf with my friend, Bobbie. However, when I was in the area, I had lunch with Andrew and his Hench people. At those lunches, we discussed the investigation and had several laughs over how we were able to get away with obvious crimes we committed and were able to look for crimes with Trump and his associates that never occurred. Plus, as I stated previously, I knew I was over my head, and if true justice was ever served, myself and other perpetrators would suffer the consequences.*

Mason: *Mr. Rosenstein, remember the Rosenbergs who were electrocuted back in 1953 for selling nuclear information to the Russians?*

Rosenstein: *Yes, I do.*

Mason: *With that in mind, did you participate in trying to invoke the 25th amendment, by having President Trump declared mentally unable to assume the duties of the President of the United States?*

Rosenstein: Yes, I did. But as I stated previously, I was joking.

Mason: You know that is sedition and treason, and given the punishment the Rosenbergs received, the penalty by law is the most severe.

Rosenstein: Are any of us going to get the death penalty from the multiple felonies we committed, including sedition and treason? Death...that could hurt.

Mason: No, Mr. Rosenstein. One of our associates, that famous author in his own mind, Steve Borovay, has a better solution. Here's Mr. Borovay to explain his concept of reopening and re-populating Alcatraz along with illustrations of what should be done to address the Crimes and Seditious and Treasonous Acts of those who need to be punished.

For those who did not read the disclaimer at the beginning of this book, here it is again:

Disclaimer: Although the book is written in a manner to show crimes of individuals who partook in the greatest attempted coup in this country's history, no matter what is written, per the 14th Amendment of the Constitution Section 1, a person is presumed innocent until proven guilty.

Chapter 18

Reopening the Rock (AKA— Alcatraz Island)

A. The Remodel:

In renovating Alcatraz to make it an active facility and more tourist-friendly, the first thing that will be done is to tear it in half, removing 50 percent of the prison cells, making it open to the public and the elements. The prisoners will suffer as it gets very cold and windy at night. But we will make sure we keep them alive if possible as they will attract more tourists than the dolphins at Sea World in San Diego. The inmates will be provided matches and sticks to light a fire at night. Boy and Girl Scouts will teach those who have no clue as to how to light a fire.

The original plumbing will be left with large fans blowing the offensive smell of these low lives back in their faces. Old light bulbs will be replaced with old energy-inefficient bulbs.

Additionally, capitalism will be on display to no end as only Rock approved cameras selling for $200, each with 24 pictures maximum, will be allowed. No electronics are permitted when visiting, and there will be countless signs requesting the tourists not to feed the ~~animals~~ prisoners.

To show our humanity, we will let the inmates have access to a porta-potty twice daily, before opening the Rock and after closing. The one porta potty will be cleaned at least one time per month. Additionally, instead of the standard prison hat and attire, prisoners will be allowed to wear a prison wardrobe of their choosing.

Legendary WWE Superstar Undertaker will serve as Warden with some of the most famous Superstars of past years serving as guards.

Here's a photo of the recycled porta potty that will be used and some of the offenders who took a shit on protecting every citizen's constitutional rights:

The Ultimate Warrior stood true to his beliefs. Prior to his early passing, he made amends with the WWE and the legends of the past. Mueller and Comey stood true to their beliefs that they were the ultimate deciders of whose constitutional rights to uphold and those who would be denied. They are two of the biggest reasons why we are in the **fine Constitutional mess** that exists today. Equal justice was never their true objective. Just ask those whose lives they have destroyed.

Here's another one of those individuals who had a *holier than thou* attitude that they are the deciders of who should be brought to justice despite no crime being committed.

As this is a horrific place to stay, those patriotic American guards of our constitutional rights violators will be able to go ashore and rest comfortably at night with two heroic American icons overseeing security from sundown to sunrise. No one will escape the Rock...

We will be placing out to bid the renovation project. However, it will take only two months as the fixes are minimal. The bids will factor out those companies that have contributed significantly to the swamp in DC.

Again, to show our humanity, prisoners will be allowed to visit each other, handcuffed and shackled for 10 minutes a day in a common area with prison guards.

Randy, *Macho Man,* Savage was incredible and a true wrestling legend. What wasn't incredible was how Weissmann and Rhee have long been a part of the deep state and how they have abused our system of justice. Weissmann was so deep state he didn't even tell Rhee he was the one who hired her only because of her legal prowess in defending the undefendable.

The incredible amount of cash awards to individuals who have broken constitutional rights of others via GoFundMe pages, book deals, speaking fees, media gigs, and other devious funding means could be the subject of another book.

President Trump and his entourage will visit the new Rock one day prior to its public opening due to security reasons. Here is a photo of President Trump and supporters of the Constitution and its Bill of Rights as they tour the facility.

For Hillary, President Trump and his entourage had to leave the cart to get a closer view of her suffering. Lt. Colonel Michael Flynn was smiling ear to ear, finally realizing justice was served equally, especially to those who sought to destroy his life.

B.   The Grand Opening

April 1st, 2021, will become a historic day for our Country as The Rock, also known as Alcatraz Island, is being reopened to house those who desecrated the Constitution and the rights of its citizens.

As the boat full of patriots reach their destination with our guide Mr. Roark, his loyal sidekick Tattoo can be heard saying:

There were an estimated 200,000 individuals gathered to hear President Trump give his speech at the reopening. During the speech, the *fake news*, represented by **Jim Acosta,** had to get their two cents in disputing the President's claim as to the size of the crowd.

Mr. McMahon, standing behind President Trump, WWE (World Wrestling Entertainment) CEO and face of the company for decades, was very unhappy about Acosta using the word *"fake."* He told the prison warden, The Undertaker, to take Acosta out with a *Tombstone Pile Driver.* It was reported that prior to this happening, infamous Civil Rights Leader, Rev. Al Sharpton, gave Acosta his last rites. The Undertaker then performed his iconic move placing Acosta's arms after the deed was done in a manner where he was resting in a coffin. The Undertaker's last words to his victim were *"Acosta, now rest in peace!"*

Jonathan: *Dad, why do you have to talk about WWE all the time?*

Jon, in wrestling entertainment, you know the good guys from the bad. Only when they either go from the good to the dark side or vice-versa, are you surprised and caught off guard. Most of the boys (or girls) participating in the coup, tried to convince those paying attention they were the good guys. I never fell for it as in my world, it was just too obvious as to what they had done.

Jonathan, additionally, we've made a ton of money off the stock, and I love watching WWE, whether on RAW, Smackdown, NXT, or the WWE Network. Plus, without all those extra funds, I could not afford your food bill of roughly five grand per month. You owe your excess weight gain to WWE.

Jonathan: *Dad, you're so old!*

I have no choice about getting old. But unless I keep making money off WWE stock, you will starve and lose tons of weight.

Jonathan: *Dad, long live the WWE!!!*

In closing his long speech at the Grand Opening of New Rock, President Trump exclaimed:

Much like the Universal City tram ride throughout the park, there will be a tour guide. Like Universal City and Disneyland, after viewing the exhibited prisoners and giving their life story, including citing the crimes they committed, there will be a souvenir gift shop to take home a remembrance of your visit. In Hillary's case, as the crimes go on into infinity, and if the guide recited all we would be hitting the 22nd Century, we will limit Hillary's crimes to 25 per tour.

Once prosecution is complete on all violators and all sentenced to a lifetime on the Rock without the possibility of parole, all evidence used in the conviction will be put up for public auction with funds going to reduce the national deficit. Items not sold will be either shredded or if electronics, demolished with a Hillary certified hammer. Replicas of each item sold will be mass-produced for sale within an Alcatraz store.

Here are some photos of people shopping at the Hillary Clinton Store called *Nick Knack Don't Get Patti Whack.*

Note to my readers: Galih, my illustrator, sent me the Nick Knack Don't Get Patti Whack drawing on July 20th, 2019. Jeffrey Epstein *allegedly committed suicide* on August 10th, 2019. It's purely coincidental the timing of this illustration. I do not need to say any more for fear of getting Patti Whacked.

Within the Clinton store, there is a section for the sale of smashed and damaged electronic devices, including cell phones and hard drives that have been cleaned *"like with a cloth."*

And then we have the Family Section where inmates share photos of their loved ones with each other.

BTW...the Eighth Wonder of the World was Andre, the Giant.

Then we have the Lovers Section:

I meant the Lovers Quarrel Section.

The New Rock will be an incredible lesson to future generations that the U.S. Constitution that forms the basis of our country should not be violated without retribution. Further, those who believe the socialist mantra that *"a particular end justifies a particular means"* will not be met with apathy but with the law of the land.

Mr. Mason and my fellow Americans, a system without accountability can only lead to the destruction of what we all hold near and dear to us.... The U.S. Constitution.

When people are not held accountable for their criminal acts with no fear of equal justice, those who want to control the levers of power manipulate those who lack the understanding and education to know they are being used to push a false narrative. The civil rights and constitutional law violations we have seen with minimal accountability will continue until the rule of law is restored. The system has failed tremendously as it has fallen to one man, Bill Barr, the Attorney General, to oversee persecution against those who have committed crimes against our constitutional rights.

C. Where is Barack?

Jonathan: *Dad, sorry to interrupt your presentation, but where is former President Obama?*

Good question, Jonathan. Conspicuously absent from incarceration is former President Barack Obama. As it turns out, prior to his arrest, he left the country and is now taking asylum in the Ecuadorian Embassy in London. This is him pictured with his cat, Satan, from his balcony, and your uncle David and his cat, Zeus, and your Cousin Joshua smoking from a bong.

Jonathan: *Dad, my cousin Joshua, doesn't do drugs?*

I know that, but Joshua is very shy and attends San Diego State University, a University known for its hot chicks. He will be the rave of the campus as these chicks will want his autograph, and his shyness will not stand in the way.

Jonathan: *Dad, that's not right, calling pretty girls hot chicks. Who do you think you are, Frank Sinatra?*

I wish Jonathan. However, I literally meant what I said:

Jonathan: *Dad, Barack Obama is from Hawaii. Some people are going to think you are saying he's not from the United States and will call you a racist?*

To those people, I say, get a life! It's satire and my world consist of rainbows of all people whose skin color is irrelevant, only the quality of their character matters. The love of my life was black, but to me, she was just Renee.

Words are important, but actions more so. Always judge a person on their actions and not solely on their words. Others will interpret the individual they hate as a threat to whatever crisis of the day they have created. It's a Saul Alinsky tactic where they manufacture a crisis to destroy the object of their despise. A checklist should be created and divided into two columns. The first column is for the words used with the second for the action by the target that justified those words.

It's multiple Saul Alinsky tactics that are being used by the haters, but none more specifically than: "*Keep the pressure on, with different tactics and actions, and utilize all events of the period for your purpose. The threat is usually more terrifying than the thing itself.*"

D. Conclusions:

Like the *Red Scare* of the 1940s and 1950s, suspension of individual civil rights and the hysteria that has been generated unjustifiably because of the desire to control the masses into believing a false narrative does no one any good.

Our system of justice is based on innocence before proven guilty. For the narrative shown above to come to fruition, the accused must be tried per the 6th amendment of the Constitution that grants criminal defendants the right to a speedy and public trial by an impartial jury consisting of jurors from the state and district in which the crime was alleged to have been committed. Under the impartial jury requirement, jurors must be unbiased, and the jury must consist of a representative cross-section of the community. The term always used is by a juror of their peers.

It would have been fitting if Benedict Arnold served as the head juror, but you can't have a traitor ruling on other traitors. It's sort of like Jeannie Rhee, Clinton Foundation, and Hillary's attorney during the email non-investigation, being appointed to find crimes against Donald Trump and his associates. A big oops! Never mind. But my choice for jurors is the Creators of our Constitution.

Hey, Jonathan, get out of the picture!

As Americans, we need to set a standard for all future generations standing for truth, justice, and the American Way! We're not perfect people, but our humanity toward others is unequaled on this planet.

Mr. Mason, I'm finished with my presentation on the New Alcatraz, The Rock, a place that houses the most despicable of all, those who did not uphold our constitutional rights.

Mason: *Thank you, Mr. Borovay, and long live the red, white, and blue.*

Schiff: We will adjourn for today.

Those are the highlights of the testimony of those who were pivotal in participating in an attempted coup. This was only the first and only day of testimony as Chairman Schiff was last seen running down the hallway of Congress with his pants on fire.

The next day, April 2nd, former Attorney General Loretta Lynch, former President Barack Obama, Hillary Clinton, and former C.I.A. Director John Brennan, were to be called to the stand. However, as Adam Schiff was a no show that day, the hearings were called off. There was rampant speculation as to where Adam Schiff was.

LIAR, LIAR PANTS ON FIRE
HOSPITAL
SCHFF, PUT ON YOUR BIG BAY PANTS & GET BACK TO DC

Chapter 19

Mueller Report – The Nuclear Fallout

Jonathan, it's difficult to believe that logic never prevailed in the MSM. The ratings of CNN and MSNBC collapsed as the lies of the Russian Hoax propaganda mongers were exposed even to the most naive people. Rachel Maddow was wearing black and in tears as she tried to get through her broadcast after the report was released. There were 10 million reasons why she kept something going that never had any grains of truth in it. One, she hated anyone who goes against the Socialist/Globalist cabal. Two, she makes $10 million dollars a year, as being a gossip columnist pays handsomely.

After that dark night, Rachel Maddow was last seen in her office looking at potential evidence to prove collusion for her next broadcast. Then she hit the jackpot as Christopher Steele emailed a picture he took of Trump enjoying the company of two of the most famous Russian spies:

The next day on Morning Joe, Mika Brzezinski and Joe Scarborough went apoplectic when reporting what Rachel uncovered the previous night:

But the Moose who knew everything about Boris and Natasha in their over 60-year relationship in their defense responded:

Similarly, after the Mueller Report release, you have talking heads of networks, such as Jeff Zucker, defending CNN's coverage telling the New York Times in an email, *"We are not investigators. We are journalists, and our role is to report the facts as we know them, which is exactly what we did."*

With that response, somewhere within the Mount Moriah Cemetery in Kansas City, Missouri, **Walter Cronkite** was spinning in his grave.

The Most Trusted Man in America once said, *"In seeking truth, you have to get both sides of a story."*

My sources of knowledge come from all forms of media. But my condemnation of this coup d'état entails not only the deep state, Obama Administration, and career bureaucrats but also mainstream Republicans including Senators Mitt Romney and Jeff Flake, along with the Republican establishment, the Never Trumpers, and all those who just can't see past their emotions. Romney added insult to injury when after reading the Mueller Report, he twittered: *"I am sickened at the extent and pervasiveness of dishonesty and misdirection by individuals in the highest office of the land, including the President.*

" I am also appalled that, among other things, fellow citizens working in a campaign for president welcomed help from Russia including information that had been illegally obtained; that none of them acted to inform American law enforcement; and that the campaign chairman was actively promoting Russian interests in Ukraine."

For someone in such a high position to be so clueless as to what transpired, the only thing I can say in his defense is he wasn't the only one *"punked"* by Mueller and his deep state operatives.

When individuals call out President Trump's lack of civility, I point to those like Mitt Romney, who had no fight for our country. As Harry Reid, with immunity on the Senate floor, questioned Romney's tax returns, book of women, and how he treated his dog, Romney stood above the fray and said nothing. How did that work out Mitt as our Constitutional Rights have been shredded and only apply to one side of the populace?

Mitt Romney went AWOL and refused to fight back against those seeking to destroy him as untrue allegations were hurled his way solely to discredit his candidacy. Instead, he decided:

The final straw was during the last debate with President Obama at Hofstra University on October 12th, 2012, when Romney failed to put Obama on the defensive on the inconsistencies of the Administration's claims on Benghazi. There was minimal confrontation as the host, CNN's Candy Crowley, sided with Obama. But the tiger in the belly of Romney was missing as he failed to make Obama account for numerous versions of what caused the attack, what Obama did while it happened, and where he and Secretary Clinton were at the time of the attack.

Finally, showing the total lack of heart he had for winning, Romney pulled a Clinton and failed to campaign in the waning days of the election in states that were up for grabs.

Unfortunately, the Republican establishment's *civility* went out the door long ago, and it's time to take off the gloves and deliver a Cassius Clay *didn't see that punch* against Sonny Liston (the Big Bear)

to destroy those evil, deep state, power-hungry, destroyers of our
Constitutional Rights.

Not coincidentally, the nickname for Russia at one time was *The
Russian Bear.*

Muhammad Ali was true to his convictions. However, during the
1960s, he was the most divisive public figure in the world with his
refusal to be drafted that cost him prime years of his boxing career.
Like Paul Robeson, he felt based on the way America has treated
blacks, *"Why should they ask me to put on a uniform and go 10,000
miles from home and drop bombs and bullets on Brown people in
Vietnam while so-called Negro people in Louisville are treated like
dogs and denied simple human rights?"* I truly admire those who
have the conviction that goes counter to groupthink and question
those in power.

Jonathan: *Dad, again not to change the subject, but what is Moe*

Jonathan, just between you and me, Moe was born in 1960 and will be celebrating his 60th birthday (434th in people years) on July 4th, 2020. My life-long friend, Dr. Ron (of Dr. Ron's Animal Hospital, the best veterinary hospital in Simi Valley, CA), gave Moe incredible care over the decades that has permitted him to live longer than father time.

Jonathan, getting back to Muhammad Ali, he was one of my all-time favorite people, like another one, Winston Churchill, who stood true to his beliefs.

The righteous indignation exhibited by the establishment Republicans, the MSM, the Democrats, and the people who are deeply rooted in our most precious institutions, is truly disgusting!

Chapter 20

I'm No Political Hack

Jonathan: *Dad, there will be those out there who claim you're in President Trump's camp.*

Jonathan, I'm the farthest thing from a political hack as Julian Assange should not be charged or persecuted like our government is trying to do.

Also, I don't see a positive end game with tariffs on China in particular. Governments who rule without a true election such as Communist or Socialist/Marxist countries are not concerned with the overall welfare of their citizens. The last time the Chinese people rose in revolt was stamped out on June 4th, 1989, incident in Tiananmen Square, where a lone protestor confronted the Chinese military sitting in a tank. As such, the masses under these people's control are never given the full explanation as to how their country is stealing the U.S. intellectual property, or how China takes advantage by manipulating their currency, or taxed the U.S. goods coming into the country to their advantage.

Additionally, as Americans, we tend to go to political extremes—from a conservative agenda under President Reagan to George W. Bush's Republican big government to Obama's big government socialist agenda to Trump's America-first policies. Chinese leaders are waiting for another President who will go in a different direction.

Finally, on tariffs, they ignore the fundamental law of Econ 101. Supply meets demand with a willing buyer willing only to pay an up to a certain amount or forgo that good. There is an economic delay in an economy feeling the effect. As once price increases, the consumer cuts back its demand, resulting in decreasing sales and a negative effect on the economy. History bears out tariff wars as a disaster, too. Several historians point to the Smoot-Hawley Tariff Act of 1930, leading to and exacerbating the Great Depression. Congress raised tariffs on over 20,000 imported products to protect domestic businesses and family farms from international trade. The results, at first, were positive. But these restrictive policies were eventually ineffective and disastrous. Unless there is some consensus in Congress on possible legislation that eliminates China's long-term game, I just don't see a positive outcome to tariffs.

There will be those who *"try to kill the messenger"* (i.e., me) as they will say I have a political agenda, and I'm a radical right-winger. That truth can quickly be dispelled as I voted for Proposition 8 in California legalizing same-sex marriages and are for the legalization of marijuana.

Jonathan: *Dad, you need to tell the readers the truth. The reason you were for permitting same-sex marriages was it opened the floodgates as to making more people unhappy like you were when you were married. You told me now 50 percent of those same-sex people will end up in divorce and join you in suffering with you saying, "Misery loves company."*

Bottom line Jonathan, I voted in favor of it. So, who cares why I did it?

I'm fiscally conservative, and on social issues, I have no problem helping those who are *unable* to help themselves. I highlighted *unable* as there are those who are able-bodied and live off government subsidies. With this dependence, it creates an electorate that favors those in power who are willing to give free stuff at the expense of future generations. The rich do not have enough wealth to pay for all the free stuff for those who have illegally come into the country and become dependent on the government.

Your mother is Mexican and legally immigrated here, and my old girlfriend, Renee, of over 10 years, is black. So, if the opposition throws out the race card, it's a fallacy.

No, Jonathan. I'm the farthest thing away from a political hack. I'm about the truth and the Constitution and the rule of law. I'm against anyone using the heavy hand of government to get back at their foes.

It's one thing enforcing the rule of law, but it's another hideous thing to distort the rule of law and use it to get back at others you view as the enemy. Then, there is a whole new level of taking government power and trying to take out of the office a sitting President who was elected by the rule of law. **Eventually, the truth will come out as Winston Churchill, who led Great Britain as Prime Minister during its *"Finest Hour"* against Nazi Germany once said:**

There are those who try to pull in historical figures and evaluate them on the PC culture of today. The only way to view anyone is in the world they lived in and what was acceptable and unacceptable, given the norms of that time.

It's a delusion used to destroy the past and make us all the same, worshipping the illusionary culture of oneness.

Chapter 21

The Hatred Runs Deep

The establishment Republicans have shown a tremendous unwillingness for defending our Constitution. Where is the outrage over the fact that the former administration and its intelligence agencies violated the constitutional rights of a candidate and his supporters perpetrating a coup to take him out of office? Why are they on a moral high ground, when those who seek to destroy have thrown all decency away? Why are they verbally attacking a President who throws political correctness aside in his battle to defend the rule of law? Where is there outrage at the comments of their own click, or the Pelosis, the Schumers, a lot of the new breed Democrats who spew hatred against our Constitution, religious freedom, those who think for themselves, and in general, seek to destroy their perceived enemies? It's time to look in the mirror and do a reality check throwing your emotions of self-righteousness aside and seeking the truth!

It was an obstruction to the nth degree by the Democrats and mainstream Republicans that contributed to a false narrative being perpetuated constantly, obstructing and diverting away from the real criminals who committed real crimes. With the Mueller Investigation turning into an act that all participants knew crimes had never been committed, we have gone into a full-fledged constitutional crisis.

As Walter Cronkite said, *you only get the truth by looking at both sides of the story,* once I did that, I saw where the truth lay. Also, I'm registered with no party affiliation, and right-wingers would hate my views on same-sex marriage, pot, and abortion.

But heads of these major networks, much like Jeff Zucker, only care about those things that bring a sitting President they despise down. The truth has no bearing on reality. It's only the reality of what reporters believe that matters. Maybe the MSM could learn something from the individual labeled the most trusted man in America... Walter Cronkite. I seriously doubt it. For the Standard Operating Procedure is once one delusion is nuked, they move quickly to the next. It's the Saul Alinsky tactic of *"keep the pressure on, with different tactics and actions, and utilize all events of the period for your purpose."* President Trump was elected more on those disillusioned by Washington D.C. and disconnect between our everyday lives and what those in power think about what is good for us. They have no clue.

Rachel Maddow got so desperate after spreading 2½ years of Trump-Russia collusion that she spread another rumor about a celebrity. On April 1ˢᵗ, 2020, she told her viewers that: *"Despite rumors to the contrary, Humpty Dumpty after his great fall, was put back together again by all the king's horses and all the king's men and is resting comfortably in Liar, Liar Pants on Fire Hospital."*

Well, despite the collusion by political opponents, deep state players who tried to tip the scales of justice, a compromised and anti-Trump special counsel and especially the MSM, who for over 2½ years peddled a scenario that from the get-go made no sense, there were holdovers who found any decision other than collusion and interference were not acceptable.

Despite the investigation by Mueller and his team of marauders, Adam Schiff still maintains that Trump colluded with Russia to win the 2016 election.

What is just as outrageous is Hillary Clinton coming out on April 23rd, 2019 telling Time Magazine: *"President Donald Trump escaped obstruction of justice charges only because of a Justice Department rule barring the indictment of a sitting president.*

"I think there's enough there that any other person who had engaged in those acts would certainly have been indicted. But because of the rule in the Justice Department that you can't indict a sitting president, the whole matter of obstruction was very directly sent to the Congress."

Clinton never stated the 10 instances Mueller gave in the second part of his report on *"Obstruction"* was based in part on information President Trump's attorneys gave in the unprecedented access Mueller and his team had as President Trump never claimed, "*executive privilege.*" Additionally, she threw out a false narrative on obstruction charges, as this has been the most effective means of diverting the attention away from crimes she committed.

However, Bill Barr, Attorney General, ordered multiple investigations that, hopefully, will lead to the arrest and imprisonment of those who sought to destroy the fundamental values of our country.

Everyone by now should get the point. Common sense should always prevail over emotion. Once you take your emotions out of the issue, it's logic that prevails. With Asperger's, it's easy for me to do for sure. For people who can't get past their hatred, the truth will never matter unless it fits their narrative.

People who hate the Constitution and the rule of law will defer, deflect, and point the finger at someone else, much like Hillary did above and continues to do so. The question is the answer in this case as these people can't answer it with the truth, or they destroy the narrative they are trying to create. I've taken the emotion out of the picture and looked at the entire situation logically. People who

committed the crimes they did thought they would never be persecuted because they were being protected by President Hillary Clinton.

To some, it was obvious it was an attempted coup d'état from the
start. However, when CIA Director John Brennan briefed the gang
of 8 in early August of 2016, it was perpetuated within our political
system as our leaders on both sides failed to exercise common
sense.

Four of the Gang of 8 included Senate Majority Leader Mitch
McConnell (R-KY), House Speaker Paul Ryan (R-WI), Senate Minority Leader Harry Reid (D-NV), and House Minority Leader
Nancy Pelosi (D-CA). All the four neglected to do any due diligence
and contributed to spreading a false narrative within the system.

Brennan again met with Reid, and for a second time, demanded he
writes a letter to the FBI, which started the ball rolling. Brennan
stated in testimony and on the *fake news* that he never saw the dossier until December of 2016. This lying traitor (appointed by
Obama), leaked bits and pieces to the press that summer to have
everyone begin to ask questions before the election. ALL
PLANNED, hoping Trump would not be elected.

The coup d'état almost perpetrated needs to be exposed, and those
who are a part of it are held accountable with consequences. But
from here on out, Jonathan, the focus needs to be on what went
wrong with the system and why we are in a constitutional crisis.

It starts with your uncle David.

Chapter 22

Uncle David and Rules for Radicals

Uncle David, because he looked so much like Karl Marx as documented in our first book, *Dad, Why Are You So Old?*, was not in the public school system until he was 11. He had no homeschooling and would watch television nonstop from the time he awoke until the time he slept. Television provided what limited education he had. He loved the commercials and would beg your grandparents to get him anything from Lucky Strike cigarettes, Schlitz Beer, RC Cola, and Oscar Meyer Weiner's. My parents knew he wasn't going to be too smart. They paid more attention to me because they knew who my father was. Uncle David's greatest ambition in life was to become an Oscar Meyer Weiner. He sang the Oscar Meyer song for years and years:

Finally, with the release of *Spartacus* in the latter part of 1960, and the courage and conviction of Kirk Douglas to go against the culture of blacklisting those who were or perceived to be Communist sympathizers, the Red cloud slowly came off. It's the Kirk Douglases of the world who risk their reputations and livelihoods that led the fight against those on either side who try to oppress.

Dalton Trumbo, a blacklisted writer during the *Red Scare*, was listed under his real name on the credits for the movie. After seeing the movie, grandpa and grandma took uncle David out of hiding. At 11 years of age, uncle David started his formal education in the 1st grade among 6- and 7-year-olds.

Uncle David enjoyed his first day in school, at least, for the first 15 minutes.

Unfortunately for uncle David, Milton Berle was considered the first major American television star and was known to millions of viewers as *"Uncle Miltie"* and *"Mr. Television"* during TV's Golden Age starting in the late 1940s.

Eventually, as your uncle couldn't keep up with the 1st graders, he was demoted to kindergarten on his second day of school. That suited him fine as his favorite class became the afternoon nap, and unlike a lot of kids in his class, he didn't have to wear diapers.

Unfortunately, uncle David was not allowed to smoke or drink beer. However, he was permitted to dress as an Oscar Meyer Weiner. Although many kids wanted to be an Oscar Meyer Weiner, it was rare they would dress up as one. But to your uncle's credit, it was better to be an Oscar Meyer Weiner than wanting to be an Anthony Weiner.

For, if he wanted to be an Anthony Weiner, he'd be singing:

> *Oh, I wish I was an Anthony Weiner,*
> *that is what I'd truly like to be,*

cause if I were an Anthony Weiner,
schoolgirls would be in love with me.

Weiner was the husband of Huma Abedin, a top aide to Hillary Clinton. He's famous for posting pictures of his private parts under an alias name of *Carlos Danger*. Due to his admission of sex crimes with a minor, he was sentenced to 21 months in prison, ordered to pay a $10,000 fine, and was required to register as a sex offender permanently. As Weiner permitted Abedin to use his laptop, Abedin used it to make copies of Clinton correspondence received from Hillary's unprotected server rooted deep in her basement at her private residence in Chappaqua, New York. After a delay and holding this information, James Comey reopened the Clinton email investigation in late October 2016 to do a very quick no harm, no foul moment exonerating her. The reason was quite simple and logical, as no one thought Clinton would lose. So Comey had a CYA (Cover Your Ass) moment, just in case he never felt he would be held accountable.

Grandpa and grandma started to worry about your uncle's development, so they took him to the school psychologist, Dr. Timothy Leary. Mr. Leary would later be known for promoting psychedelic drugs (mostly LSD) and the *"turn on, tune in, drop out"* counter-culture of the 1960s.

After completing a psychological eval, Dr. Leary believed uncle David was suffering a disorder that would go away with the use of marijuana. The teacher at first was appalled, but eventually got used to the smell as did the other kindergarteners.

By the time he was 18, uncle David had graduated High School on time and started his freshmen year at San Fernando Valley College, later to be known as California State University Northridge. Due to his pot dependence, uncle David became friends with many on the far left who believed Revolution and overthrowing our Government and spreading the wealth around was the only way to solve the nation's woes.

Uncle David joined an organization called the Community Service Organization (CSO) in Los Angeles. CSO is well known for teaching others the Saul Alinsky ways, such as Cesar Chavez and Dolores Huerta. Cesar Chavez was an American labor leader and civil rights activist who, with Dolores Huerta, co-founded the National Farm Workers Association in 1962. Chavez groups used peaceful methods to protest for higher wages for farm laborers and discourage the use of illegals who took his constituents' jobs and resulted in lower wages.

Uncle David was an enthusiastic participant protesting with any anti-establishment group. Whether it was against Bank of America's support of the Vietnam War to black students takeover of the Administration Building at San Fernando Valley State College in 1969, he was there front and center.

Jonathan, that's why uncle David is the way he is. He hates everything Trump, and that goes against the socialist/globalist movement of groupthink.

Jonathan: *Dad, I feel sorry for uncle David.*

Don't feel sorry for him. He's one of the 0.1 percent and can afford to live in his own world as he's insulated from reality. With Socialism, it's *do as I say, not as I do.* The wall at his private residence shows how he protects himself from what he supports:

Jonathan *Dad, you're right. Uncle David is a Socialist/Globalist at heart if he can keep his wealth using any means to protect it from those who pose a threat.*

After graduating from college in 1972, uncle David went from participating in community organizing to indoctrinating professors in the ways of Saul Alinsky. A Master of Teaching how to spread a false narrative (the means) to achieve a desired result (the ends), uncle David taught college professors how to control the thought processes of the most vulnerable (the young and unknowing). To this day, the results of uncle David's college organizing are seen throughout the country on campuses with safe spaces, where individuals who think differently are physically attacked (Antifa) or silenced from expressing views outside the mantra of groupthink and where emotions override commonsense.

As time went by, uncle David, eventually got a job as a CPA in the private sector, invested in stocks (with my help and money), became a multi-millionaire and a Socialist/Globalist if it didn't affect his wealth which is attributed to his capitalism.

Although your uncle is now a shadow of his former self, there are those out there who have carried on his banner of hatred of our Constitution and all it stands for. *"Burn baby, burn,"* was the mantra of the 1960s. Now the radical left has invaded the system and worked from within as Saul Alinsky once wrote to control our daily lives.

Jonathan: *Dad, not to change the subject, but in the picture of an illegal climbing the wall, you let uncle David kill our friend Raul?*

Jonathan, I didn't kill him. If you look closely at the picture, the bullets are deflecting off his bulletproof sombrero. I couldn't kill one of the main characters in prior and future books. But I was mad at him, as his pig dog, Lola, pooped on my office carpet, and he refused to pick it up.

Raul is alive and starting to do better, as the impact from the bullet knocked him off his ladder and unconscious. Unfortunately, uncle

David thought he was dead and had his *corpse* transferred to the streets of San Francisco by his henchmen. It was dumped right in the open among the homeless, used needles and shit that lines the streets of this once magnificent city. San Francisco, the once glorious place on the hill and where the golden sun shined for me, has now replaced Haiti as the shit-hole of the world. Sorry President Trump, I disagree with you again.

It was business as usual until Raul awoke. Unfortunately, uncle David's enforcers dumped him right on an unused syringe of heroin. Raul spent two months in rehab and was last spotted at a Tony Bennett concert at a high-end venue in San Francisco with his pig dog, Lola.

Tony Bennett is the last of the Sinatra generation, a brilliant entertainer and great all-around person. Hopefully, one day, he can perform in *the Golden City by the Bay* without his fans having to wear clothespins on their noses.

After this incident, uncle David freaked out as he thought he killed an illegal and would be prosecuted to the nth degree. He knew if it was a citizen he murdered, he would have no problem. Uncle David decided to pay top dollar to protect all that was his from outsiders (i.e., and the California Assembly) who needed his money to give illegals free stuff (medical care, education, driver's licenses, and American jobs) and building a train to nowhere.

Although due to heavy use of pot during his younger years, uncle David was slowly realizing that with Socialism, you get open borders and illegals flooding in, uncontrolled outbreaks of diseases among the homeless, increases in crime, high net-worth individuals leaving the state in droves, bullet trains that go nowhere and the list of stupid stuff that goes on with Socialism to infinity. Maybe, one day, uncle David and I can sit down, and reason will prevail. Jonathan, until that time, I believe it's too late for uncle David as he's become too catlike like his true and only cat love, Zeus.

Cats are socialistic animals, unlike dogs. Cats have a sense of entitlement and keep to themselves in their aloofness that brings them to their servants only until they need to be fed. Every so often, they will throw their peons a Marie Antoinette *piece of cake* in the form of a dead bird or rat. Cats lack empathy as you could be lying in a pool of your own blood, and their only thought is, *"Wow, does this mean I'm not going to be fed?"*

Dogs, on the other hand, are a creation of God (dog spelled backward). Dogs are participants, not looking for free handouts and work for their treats. They eat with the common man and will protect you, like Moe, from evil. They sense when you have been hurt and will lick your wounds. I could write a book on the differences between these two totally different species. George Carlin, who had an incredible sense of human nature, spelled out the differences brilliantly as only a comic genius could.

Finally, a recent Gallop Poll found 95 percent of the cat population supporting the views of Bernie Sanders and Alexandria Ocasio-Cortez. Need I say more?

Jonathan, it's always the ones at the top of the Socialist pyramid who benefit from capitalism, taking wealth from their constituents to live a Socialist free life. It's the rap song by 2 Chainz, Big Sean and Nicki Minaj that is your uncle David's moto living it each day to the fullest on other people's money...

The YouTube video of your uncle, the Socialist/Globalist, singing *Big Socialist Bank Take Lil Socialist Bank*, went viral. As young people have a 40 percent favorable view on Socialism, it was the rave of the young socialists in our country who couldn't hesitate to destroy the concept of capitalism and promote a movement that has no successful basis in reality.

Jonathan: *Dad, not to change the subject again, but why is my trainer, Tia, standing in uncle David's socialist music video on top of the jeep? Isn't she a capitalist?*

Jonathan, she is. The only way she would have appeared in the video was she had to be paid, *"BIG BANK."*

Then Kanye West saw the video and twittered his thoughts that ran counter to the groupthink mentality by encouraging young people to think for themselves. Those enemies of free thought provided a psychological analysis of West, much like they do of President Trump, and failed to acknowledge the *Goldwater Rule*. Colluding in the analysis with the MSM that Kanye needed psychological help was **Michael Avenatti** (coined *Creepy Porn Lawyer* by Tucker Carlson). Later that night, hosts Jimmy Kimmel and Stephen Colbert reiterated the plea for Kanye to seek mental help. Meanwhile, as this was all transpiring, Bernie Sanders was resting comfortably in one of his four houses.

The Goldwater Rule was the informal name referred to in section 7 in the American Psychiatric Association Principles of Medical Ethics. When Barry Goldwater (Senator from AZ) ran against Lyndon Johnson in 1964, a psychological evaluation with no credibility was portrayed all over the media that Goldwater was a lunatic. This culminated with an iconic pro-Johnson commercial of an atomic bomb going off in the background as a young girl was playing in a field. This rule made it unethical for psychiatrists to give a professional opinion about public figures whom they have not examined in person, and from whom they have not obtained consent to discuss their mental health in public statements. Wow, how times have changed.

Funny how the MSM had Michael Avenatti as their go-to guy on the crimes of Trump and his associates (121 times on CNN and 133 times on other MSM outlets), never having performed their psychological analysis on a guy whose only qualities in their eyes was his hatred of Donald Trump, and how he articulated that in the groupthink strategy of the MSM in destroying President Trump. Brian Seltzer, the host of CNN Reliable Sources, even said to Avenatti that he could be a 2020 Presidential Candidate, *"based on your presence on cable news."*

There was only one question the MSM had to ask the *"Creepy Porn Lawyer"* if they even dared to vet his credibility, and that is, *"Why is Stormy Daniels, at age 39, still stripping?"* The alleged crimes of Avenatti are being exposed as his former MSM allies seek another credible stooge to lead the charge on destroying all things Trump. Obviously, the Goldwater Rule applied to Avenatti for the MSM, but not to those they hate.

Jonathan, it was that simple. Common sense, tone down your emotions and drill down to the facts, and almost everything in life is easier to explain. We both have Asperger's, so emotions are easily suppressed, and our brains are wired to think logically. Although at the time I married your mother, I didn't know what I was thinking.

Kanye West, like all those who dare to stand up and go against groupthink, lays true to the foundation of conviction as Martin Luther King Jr. once proclaimed:

Kanye dared to speak out against those who tell us how to think and knew he would be ostracized for doing so. Hats off to you, Kanye... except, I must always wear a hat due to my propensity for skin cancer on my head.

Jonathan, furthermore, **I do not know the beliefs of 2 Chainz, Big Sean, or Nicki Minaj, but their music along with their counterparts Kanye, Cardi B, Blue Face, and Tyga just hit the right spot for me.**

There is nothing better than me riding in my 1981 Toyota Corolla with the two doggies, Moe and Maisy, you and Tia bebopping and twerking to Tyga's classic: *"Stick Out Ya Tongue, Girls Want to Have Fun"*:

Note to Child Services: When my illustrator, Galih, drew Jonathan smoking a doobie, Jon was 18. So, we're cool, right Snoop?

Much like Elvis hip gyrations in the 1950s, the moral outrage to words and body movements of these very talented individuals defines their generation along with a wide variety of different genres of music. It's only words, and as I'm old school, very old school, *"actions mean more than words."* Also, I'm probably the only 60 something that loves rap.

Jonathan: *Dad, there aren't many of you left, so what are you talking about, maybe out of 100 people?*

Jon, I still can't believe 35 different blood tests showed I'm still your father.

Jonathan: *Dad, you also used the 'N' word in the panel above. You can't do that as you're not black.*

Jonathan, who are you, the PC police? Not that it matters, but that's the words sung by Tyga coming out of my radio. I'm too busy bebopping to the lyrics to sing. Anyway, with that, you lose your allowance!

Jonathan: *For asking a question, you take away my allowance? How am I going to buy food at McDonald's? That's not fair!*

Jon, life's not fair, and I just **Alinskied** you. I diverted, redirected, and pointed a finger back at you. See it works.

When the younger generation shows their parents the Tyga music video, they will probably be grounded with cell phone privileges revoked. In the meantime, fathers, due to the nature of men, will probably watch this video in private of these incredible young ladies twerking.

But the bottom line, again, is that they are only words and post-Elvis type moves. It should be noted a number of these rappers give back big time to the community. If you judge a person by their words instead of their actions, what would you think about an unnamed President saying to the UK, he likes that guy when removing the Churchill statute from the White House? This is the same President, who, when visiting Jerusalem, stated he considers himself the first Jewish President. This was despite the fact this President had an 8 percent approval rating in Israel, the lowest of any President since Israel's statehood in 1948. Always judge a person by their actions. If their words live up to their actions, that shows someone with enough conviction to carry through on their promises.

Music and talent exceed by far whatever anyone's personal beliefs are or the words they use in their songs. Neil Young prevented his song, *"Rockin in the Free World,"* from closing Trump rallies. Although Young is a supporter of Bernie Sanders, the anti-thesis of a free world, his music transcends generations. He, along with Jagger and Richards, are the greatest writers of music of all time. I hope Neil keeps *rockin* for a long time to come.

There's no greater victim of the socialist/globalist/groupthink mentality than my friend Stephanie. Her emotions are based on what people say and run counter to the old saying, "*Actions mean more than words.*"

Jonathan, she is a blatant example of how ignorance can destroy a society.

Chapter 23

Cow Flatulence and My Hot Socialist Friend

Jon, do you remember in my last book I talked about the friend who comes over who has been contaminated on her path to adulthood?

Jonathan: *Yeah, dad. You told me you never wanted me to meet her because she's an idiot and will poison my mind.*

Unfortunately, the millennials and your generation are getting the full thrust of socialism as an accepted norm. My friend, Stephanie, is a prime example of the teachings in school, what the mainstream media feeds them, and how those who differ from groupthink need to be silenced.

For those who have problems with their eyesight, President Obama is saying to a large crowd, "*If you believe the other side, that chicken over there, next to the little girl and her cat, is a duck. But we all know just because it walks like a duck, talks like a duck, it isn't a duck, it's a chicken.*"

Jonathan, that's socialism. A justified false means equals the desired end as you clothe the means in moral garments. It's a Saul Alinsky tactic that Barack Obama used to convince the unknowing by constant repetition of a lie, making it at the end an accepted truth.

Everything Socialists stand for they defend by pulling a card from their deck of rhetoric and use their emotion to discredit the opposition. Whether it's Russian collusion, sexual allegations, or race, there's a card in the deck that they pound into our heads as a false truth. If the next Trump Supreme Court nominee is a woman, my longtime friend, Constitutional Karl, firmly believes it's the race card from the deck of lies they will pull out.

When Obama and his supporters repeatedly tried to take credit for an economy they never had under his administration, I would ask Stephanie, *"what are his policies or executive orders that caused this to happen?"* Crickets and more crickets. What the MSM and those who support Socialism/Globalism always refuse to do is to drill down to the specific facts, the numbers, the policies, and anything that shows how Obama is responsible for this improvement.

That night for dinner, I prepared Stef a meal consisting of fried crickets sautéed in feces of rats with a dessert of chocolate fried ants. Socialism/Globalism is nothing more than sugar-coated pestilence.

My friend, Stephanie, is now an ancient 27. Her new favorite socialist is Alexandra Ocasio-Cortez (aka AOC), elected to the House of Representatives (D-New York) in the 2018 election. Stefanie loves the lady so much that she has a tattoo of her on her back, along with her other favorite socialists.

Ocasio-Cortez announced her New Green Deal in February 2019 to get rid of greenhouse gases in a 10-year period by eliminating airplanes and cars and only having trains. Further, she wants to re-build every building in this country to make them green energy efficient. She also wants to give everyone a living wage whether they want to work or not. Finally, she wants to eliminate cows whose flatulence contributes to poisonous gases in the air.

When I asked Stephanie to back up the fact that bovines contributed significantly to greenhouse gases, she could only say, *"Well, that's what Ocasio-Cortez said."* Ocasio-Cortez based her beliefs on data used in the Paris Climate Agreement, where dissenters were not given a voice.

It's difficult to believe cows that descended from the wild ox over 10,500 years ago are now a primary source of the global warming problem. From everything I read on the statistical data used to prove warming is happening, the dissenters, who are silenced by the Globalists, say the parameters of the stats used confirming warming are so broad purposely to reflect that global warming is a fact.

Stephanie was so intent on the destruction of the bovine population that late at night, she would sneak off to pastures in the San Fernando Valley picking off cows with an AK-45. She was so concerned with the political optics, that when killing the bovines, she did it according to the ratio of the color of the cow. She was concerned that if she picked off too many black cows relative to brown and white ones, the **BCLM** (Black Cows Lives Matter) group would find her and show their displeasure by setting her house on fire, lighting cow flatulence with a match.

Jonathan: *Dad, that's insane! Why do you hang out with such an idiot?*

Jon, she's hot, and I'm shallow!

Anyway, every time she killed a cow, it made her prouder that she was doing her best to prevent global warming. As Stephanie is a globalist, she does not believe in any borders and is against a wall separating Mexico from the U.S. as a deterrent. She feels there are smarter and modern ways to deter illegals from entering our country. In her mind, a wall is nothing less than immoral. Where have I heard that before? From individuals trying to program us into groupthink, taking their word as the gospel. That is the extreme danger Ocasio-Cortez poses, as what she says seems very sincere and the best for all. But the strange thing is there is never any detail on how it's going to be paid for other than taxing the rich and printing more money, as nothing she suggests is practical and common sense.

Then I came up with a brilliant idea. I told Stephanie maybe all cows can be lined up at the border, stretching from one end to the other, enclosed in stalls. Their flatulence can act as a deterrent and send illegal aliens back to where they came from, or even better yet, killing those that traffic drugs into our country and MS-13 members. Believe it or not, Jonathan, she was excited beyond belief and wrote Ocasio-Cortez a letter with a picture drawn in crayons of the new border wall. She even added that to prevent the gases entering the United States side, they can have all cows facing the United States with their behinds facing Mexico. Additionally, her brilliant mind came up with the idea that windmills should be erected to make sure the gases do not blow back into the United States.

Jonathan: *Dad, is Stephanie dumber than a rock?*

Jon, don't insult the rock. In any event, she looks better in a bikini than a rock.

Surprisingly, Stef received a *thank you* letter from Ocasio-Cortez, giving a thumbs up to her plan with her close friends who are also in support of the Green New Deal.

Jonathan: *Dad, did Ocasio-Cortez really do that?*

Here's the picture Ocasio-Cortez mailed back...

Jonathan: *Dad, without cows, there would be no hamburgers, and thus, no McDonald's?*

Jon, corporate America is smart enough to get around the elimination of cow flatulence. **The difference between socialism and capitalism is that socialism has no profit motive and only wants to take. Capitalism, needing profitability to stay in business, figures it out.** Trust me, McDonald's will find a way.

It's almost impossible to have a civil conversation with a Socialist due to their emotions overtaking practicality. It doesn't fit a narrative that the Socialists/Globalists push to exercise more and more control over our daily lives in the name of the common good. You know this country is in a dangerous position when you take as the gospel truth something someone says without proof.

Because Stef went to San Diego State University, her indoctrination was complete. It was like the movie *Invasion of the Body Snatchers*, where logic escaped her. She was always on the attack, seeking to eat other people's brains for them to think (or not think) like her and her comrades.

I thought maybe my language and logic were too difficult for her to understand. So, I broke Socialism down in a manner Stef and her comrades (the *"useful idiots"*) could comprehend:

With that, Stephanie left in a huff. She felt I was insulting her intelligence by using an iconic monster she grew up with to prove a point.

With Socialism, there is never a cost—only tax the rich and place increased burdens on the middle class. Despite the fact there is a limited supply of doctors and medical professionals, only so much money, and only so many teachers, the laws of supply and demand never fall within the logic of those who want everything to be free.

But like most socialists, they strive for a fair society and haven't learned the lessons from history. With them, "It's *this time will be different.*" But there is no one who can say these Socialists ever made life better for their constituents.

These individuals despise any written document that defines the rules of society other than what's evolved from the *Communist Manifesto* to Alinsky tactics to present-day radicalism unfettered.

They don't believe in logical solutions; all they believe in is just a power grab.

These individuals are so reprehensible they would even protest Moses coming down Mt. Sinai:

Here's the layout of the above for those who can't read the fine print (i.e., old people):

I'm in the middle holding up our previous two books *Dad, Why Are You So Weird?* and *Dad, Why Are You So Old?*. Joe Biden is smelling Kamala Harris's hair saying, *"Kamala, your hair smells incredible."* Harris is throwing **Alinsky's** book *Rules for Radicals* shouting out to me, *"Capitalist White Man!"* Next to her is Pete Buttigieg throwing the *Rules for Radicals* book squealing at me, *Capitalist, Elitist, Non-Gay, White Male!"* Next to me, on the right, is Bernie Sanders throwing his book the *Communist Manifesto*, defiling me saying, *"Capitalist Pig, I need your money to buy my 5th house!"*

Next to Bernie, is American Indian, Elizabeth Warren. Elizabeth is just shooting an arrow directly at me degrading my color by exclaiming, *"Capitalist Paleface!"* Then there is Adolf throwing his book, *Mein Kampf,* in a hysterical rant crying out to me, *"Capitalist Jew!"*

Jonathan, all those people above are practicing identity politics and/or identity hate. In my mind, it always starts with the word *American.* Those who start first with their identity and/or hate instead of *American* lose me as it's an Alinsky tactic of *"Pick the target, freeze it, personalize it, and polarize it."* Their tactics are only a way of dividing us further and giving them more power to control.

Jonathan: *Dad, but you are a capitalist?*

An American Capitalist. I'm not going to apologize as it has worked for me with the hope that the countless masses realize how those politicians above are trying to control your thoughts by making empty promises. Plus, after 4 books and 6 years, this is the first real attempt I've made in trying to promote my books.

Jonathan: *Dad, why is Bernie Sanders throwing the book, Communist Manifesto instead of the Alinsky book?*

As the *Manifesto* was written in 1848 and Alinsky's book in 1971, I chose the book closest to his birthday.

Jonathan: *And why isn't Elizabeth Warren throwing a book?*

As she's an American Indian, tribal law applies to her beliefs. But in her defense, she comes out against the privileged white man, in support of free things for the poor and much of the same agenda preached by Ocasio-Cortez and members of her tribe.

To believe any of the above and Ocasio-Cortez's ideas are the exception to the rule has no basis in logic and is grounded in emotion. It would be the same thing to believe the dictator in Venezuela, Nicolas Maduro, can change the country from the depths of despair he took it back to one of the wealthiest in South America. The analogy is that the ideologies of all the above is for Government control of our lives to benefit the masses.

Jonathan, the inherent truth in all their rhetoric is that it seeks to divide us further. **When anyone uses as their platform *social justice* and the cries in the panel above, it escapes me. It's like Martin Luther King, Jr. in his *I Have a Dream Speech* most eloquently said:**

The proof in the pudding is that the love of my life was black. That never mattered, as I've never known a person with such love in her heart and would blink an eye to sacrifice her own life to make it better for those she cared for...and she did.

Chapter 24

If the World Is Ending, Let's Party Like It's 1999

It's ignorance that leads to those adopting a philosophy that has never worked. The Green New Energy Deal proposed by Ocasio-Cortez as a new Congresswoman gives government control of all forms of transportation, our medical care by eliminating health insurance carriers, tears down buildings that will be rebuilt to meet guidelines of energy efficiency as determined by our government, provides funds for those unwilling to work, and eliminates all cows from the face of the planet. The cost to us?

Not only are there no fiscal numbers Ocasio-Cortes uses to support the Green New Deal, Ocasio-Cortez said on January 22, 2019, at a Martin Luther King celebration event, *"The world is gonna end in 12 years if we don't address climate change, and your biggest issue is how are we gonna pay for it?"*

So, I asked my friend Stephanie if Ocasio-Cortez's plan will work over 10 years and we are the only country to follow it, how do we avoid the destruction of the planet in 12 years as major climate violators like China are still polluting? Her response was, *"Well, we need to do our share, and maybe that will give us a couple of extra months of life."* I was flabbergasted by her ignorance as even if she cared about numbers, she would have seen that we are only 5 percent of the world population. So common sense, which Stephanie lacks, says if only 5 percent of the world's population implements the Green New Energy Deal, what difference will it make if we do our share while 95 percent of the world is still polluting?

Jonathan, I probably won't be around in 12 years, and if I do pass before, you will no longer have to clean your room, as the world is coming to an end anyway. **In any event, if the world is ending in 12 years, we should party with Prince like it's 1999:**

With 1999 becoming the year 2000, out went the doomsday scenario that computer systems will crash, known as the Y2K crisis. Guess what? We're still here...

In March 2019, Greenpeace Co-Founder, Dr. Patrick Moore wrote that AOC's plan will kill everything on earth calling her *"a pompous little twit."*

Stephanie's response is how sincere she is in showing complete ignorance. Her reasoning on the Green New Deal was, *"Why would over 100 Democrats support her plan unless it would work?"*

On March 12th, 2019, President Trump tweeted that *"Patrick Moore, co-founder of Greenpeace: The whole climate crisis is not only* **fake news**, *it's* **Fake Science**. *There is no climate crisis, there's weather and climate all around the world, and, in fact, carbon dioxide is the main building block of all life."*

Google afterward deleted references of Patrick Moore as a Co-Founder of Greenpeace. This is just one of the millions of examples of groupthink as it defeats the narrative the Socialists/Globalists want you to believe. The truth becomes what they want you to think. Any opposition is eliminated, so it's never in your thought process. How is a young college student to know what their professors refuse to share, and the MSM continues to pound in your head that dissenters are ignorant, racists, homophobes, sexists, etc., etc....

Because of my Asperger's, I tend to excel at anything involving numbers. As such, I've been extremely successful in the stock market because of my numerical ability and common sense. Where are the numbers to show the real cost benefits of open borders and the financial costs of illegals have on both federal and state governments? Where are the numbers to support the point that federally controlled health care is the most effective way of providing health care from a quality and cost-benefit analysis? Where are the numbers to support the argument that global warming will destroy the planet within 12 years? What policies or executive orders specifically did President Obama implement that contributed to one of the best economies in my lifetime? The list goes on about what the group thinkers want us to believe without verification.

Jonathan, just one simple question directly answered by those trying to sell fantasies (i.e., Socialistic policies), shows there is no drill down. The easy and accurate answers, such as what did Obama do to contribute to a greatly improved economy they can never answer. The reason it improved dramatically was President Trump eliminated unneeded regulations that only served to increase the power of the federal government and burden businesses. Furthermore, lowered tax rates made the U.S. more competitive globally.

Why would they want to tell the truth when their only objective is power and control...along with the money that goes their way because of it.

The U.S. Postal Services has lost billions of dollars over the years, while competitors such as Federal Express and UPS have made tons of money. The government could care less about profitability with very little accountability to the taxpayers. Public trading companies must give an account to the shareholders of the company, with continual negative returns met with firings. It's still difficult to fire government employees due to incompetence. The big government/socialist/globalist mantle is to empower the government more without fiscal responsibility. Margaret Thatcher, former British Prime Minister, once said, *"The problem with Socialism is eventually you run out of other people's money."*

Chapter 25

The Cost of Free Stuff and A Thrill Up My Leg

It's ignorance that leads to the support of the Socialist agenda. Jonathan, to get past the emotion, you need to ask the person the facts behind what they are saying. More importantly, ask them the numbers that support their argument. There is never any drill down on how they are going to pay for their agenda other than additional taxes.

It seems the history of our country is lost on our young. I asked Stephanie if she knew who said:

After showing her the picture above, without the words drawn by my illustrator, she finally responded, *"Abraham Lincoln?"*

Jonathan: *Dad, your friend is really an idiot? I mean that in a kind way.*

Jonathan, Stephanie learned ignorance in school and by what she sees on all forms of media. Stephanie hasn't grown as a person and still has the same mentality she had 5 years ago when I met her. When questioning her on how she matured since our first encounter, she responded, *"I'm 360 degrees different."*

Jonathan: *Dad, has Stephanie ever had her head examined?*

She did, and the MRI showed nothing.

Stephanie was a bit perturbed afterward. I had to tell her about John F. Kennedy and stated when Alexandria Ocasio-Cortez becomes President, she will say:

The mantra is t*ax the rich more, increase income tax, create a net worth tax, and increase the estate tax.* Stef was thoroughly indoctrinated in a mentality where her brain had no room for the truth. The end justifies any means no matter what the cost.

Unfortunately, the history I know is no longer taught in school. In 7th grade history class, I did a report on Winston Churchill. Churchill led Great Britain during its *Greatest Hour* against the threat of Nazi Germany. We learned about the history and evils of socialism. Today, colleges, for the most part, preach the good of the philosophy. If history were a lesson, professors would have shown what **Churchill saw firsthand with Socialism. He once said, that** *"Socialism is a philosophy of failure, the creed of ignorance, and the gospel of envy; its inherent virtue is the equal sharing of misery."*

My friend Stephanie is the poster child of ignorance. I wanted to dump her, but afterward, I realized I was not with her due to her mental (or lack of) capacity.

Jonathan: *Dad, has anyone ever told you you're shallow?*

All the time, Jon. Stephanie believes everything she hears repeatedly on CNN and MSNBC, as they repeat the themes of all who seek to destroy our Constitution. She sincerely believes Donald Trump and his supporters are racists, homophobes, xenophobes, and anti-everything Socialism stands for. The playbook is obvious, and the cards they pull out in the name of control distort the truth. It's impossible for those who don't know they have been brainwashed to believe what has transpired. The indoctrination never calls out those Stef supports who meet with Louis Farrakhan or Rev. Al Sharpton. It's all one-sided, and unless they seek the truth, it's never found in the echo chamber of their existence.

Jonathan: *Dad, who is Al Sharpton?*

Jonathan, there's not even time or space in this book to drill down on this man. But he's as connected to those in Congress and haters of Jews and Israel as anyone other than Louis Farrakhan could be. Do your own homework on him, as you will see his affiliations are much like our former President Barack Obama's (with Sharpton, a frequent visitor to Obama's White House). But it doesn't matter on Stef's side as it deflects from their group message of hate.

Stephanie loves Rachel Maddow and her conspiracy theories. Her favorite guest is Michael Moore. Moore's favorite Democratic Party member is obviously Alexandria Ocasio-Cortez. He calls her the new face of the party. I thoroughly enjoy watching Rachel when Michael Moore is on. It's like a finding Waldo book:

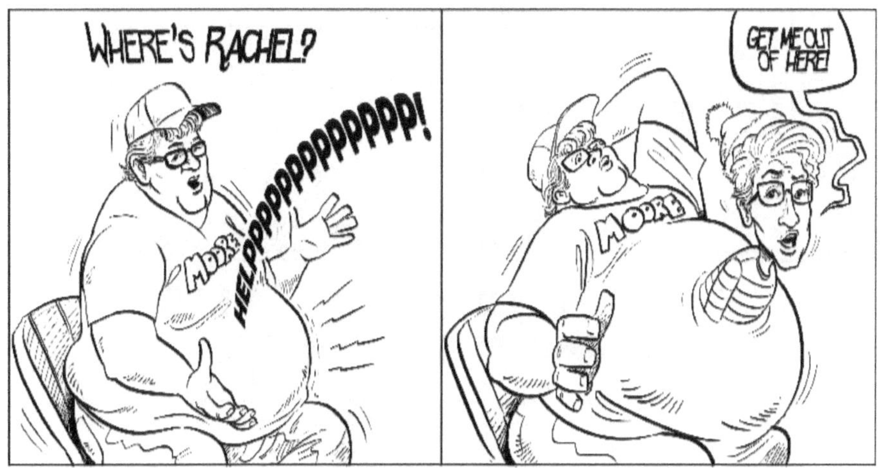

To Moore's credit, he has lost a lot of weight and, hopefully, lives a long and healthy life despite obvious mental deficiencies. Later, I found the reason for losing half his weight was his wife divorced him, and she took half of him in the settlement. I wish I could say the same about you, Jonathan, as far as losing weight.

Jonathan: *Dad, my typical reply, as outlined in our first book, to which you never have a response, Dad, why are you so old?*

In addition to Maddow, Stephanie has a crush on another old man, **Chris Matthews.** She has a poster on her bedroom wall of Matthews after an Obama primary victory speech on February 13th, 2008, saying, *"I felt this thrill going up my leg."* I showed Stef the panel my illustrator drew that Matthews meant to say, *"He had a tinkling feeling going down his leg,"* and here's the reason why:

Stephanie tried to attack Moe after seeing what really transpired, but Moe fought back, going for her ankles.

Moe made sure Matthews, a long-distance runner back in his days at the University of North Carolina at Chapel Hill, had that *tinkling feeling going down his leg* until Obama finally left o*ffice on January 19ᵗʰ, 2017.*

In the eight years Moe stalked Matthews, Matthews went through on average 270 pairs of pants a year. On the positive side, Matthews was able to lose over 80 pounds and get back to his college weight.

Chapter 26

How Anger Controls Socialist Thoughts

To show my friend Stef how she has been brainwashed, we talked about *Christine Blasey-Ford's* sexual allegations against Judge Kavanaugh. Stephanie didn't even realize she was being manipulated by those who want to control her thought processes. The objective of the haters was to defeat a judge that would throw the balance of the court off with 5 conservatives to 4 liberals.

Despite the fact that even Blasey-Ford's best friend, could not collaborate her *alleged rape* story, there were four others who were interviewed under oath who couldn't confirm any part of Ford's story. However, in Stephanie's mind, it was a confirmed fact.

The MSM repetition of *the rape* (aka Alinsky style), was an example of how a myth became a reality. Then, I went into the history of the woman's political past, showing her information that Blasey-Ford is a radical pro-abortion supporter and Clinton backer, as were her Democratic activists attorneys. Nothing seemed to matter other than she believed her. Again, emotions of anger prevailed over logic.

In my mind, it was as simple as Blasey-Ford being pro-abortion, a political activist, and very liberal for understanding Kavanaugh's nomination to the Supreme Court throwing the balance to the conservatives. Kavanaugh was presumed guilty by those who hated his legal decisions. He's anti-abortion and just the fact he was selected by President Trump. There are two sets of standards as to whom the Constitution applies and does not apply to. Those in power seek to rule with rhetoric and not facts that would not fit their narratives.

The system of justice broke down as people who face no legal consequences because they are on the correct side of the political spectrum can spew lies. Judge Kavanaugh suffered irreparable harm to his reputation that he spent decades building up—only on allegations. Although I was not thrilled with President Trump's nomination of Kavanaugh and would have selected two of the other candidates mentioned, Judge Kavanaugh stayed true to his convictions and stood against the outrageous indignation of those who hate.

The #MeToo movement was created as a result of Donald Trump. Unfortunately, due to the hatred of the man, it threw a blanket over all those they opposed, and the old saying, by Geoffrey Chaucer (an English poet and author back in the 1300s), *"People who live in glass houses, shouldn't throw rocks,"* came back *bigly* to bite them in the ass. The victims of this movement were those who have been abused. Their stories are now cast against the blanket of hate one segment of the population throws against those they oppose. The real victims of sexual abuse will never be given justice as everything Trump has been vilified to the point words matter over facts.

Jonathan: *Dad, as you are very old, did you know Chaucer like you knew Fred and Barney?*

Jon, can't you ever be serious?

Frequently, Stephanie hung the phone up on me as she has no facts to counter my view of the world, only rhetoric. In college, she never had to deal with those who have opposing views. In real life, she needs a safe space to be free of those who destroy her vision of reality.

Then there was the time, I wore an Obama *Hope and Change* tee shirt. Stephanie was smiling ear to ear as she thought I had finally seen my evil ways. It would have been the easiest way to close the evening as I would have had a great time doing other things with her that brought only pleasure. But I couldn't leave well enough alone. I explained what Obama meant and did while he was President to *"fundamentally change"* our Republic into a Socialist/Marxist/Globalist country.

Well, if sex was my end goal for that evening, I then put on my red **Make America Hat,** and Stef went ballistic! I was then called everything that involves hatred. Two hours later, after she collapsed from her verbal assault on me, I told her the truth about the saying. Explaining that Ronald Reagan first used it in his 1980 campaign, then Bill Clinton in a 1992 campaign rally, finally culminating in using it in a radio commercial that aired in support of Hillary's 2008 Presidential campaign bid. Stef was speechless.

Jonathan: *Dad, you should break up with her and go back to my mother.*

Jonathan, that will never happen. For, your mother is too old and broken down. If she was a horse, her name would be *Elmer.*

Jonathan, stop distracting me from my purpose for writing this book...to save our country. I don't want to expend more energy than I have, as it takes a lot to salvage our Constitution and what's left of our country. Your mother is the last one I want to talk about.

At President Trump's State of the Union Speech on February 5th, 2019, he stated, *"Here, in the United States, we are alarmed by new calls to adopt socialism in our country. America was founded on liberty and independence—not government coercion, domination, and control. We are born free, and we will stay free."*

Trump declared, *"Tonight, we renew our resolve that America will never be a socialist country."*

Bernie Sanders was not too happy as our President confidently stated, *"We will never be a Socialist Country."* Most members of the Democratic Party refused to stand as others stood and proudly applauded. The sight was terrifying as I realized how far this country's common sense has been tossed aside, and socialism is spreading.

Bernie Sanders became the unofficial leader of the Socialist movement in this country, indoctrinating the already indoctrinated young mind into thinking everything should be free, including *health care, education, housing,* and to all, whether legal or illegal to the country.

But the fundamental truth that most times is so apparent to me is when I asked Stephanie, *"What's the difference between all the free stuff that these Democratic Socialists want, and what's going on in California?"* Her only response, *"Well, it will be different this time."*

Chapter 27

California, Here We Go

Victor Davis Hanson, Ph.D., Senior Fellow at the Brookings Institute (lifelong Californian) and noted author, in a column in National Review on June 18th, 2019 wrote:

"Almost a quarter of the population lives below the poverty line. Another fifth is categorized as near the poverty level — facts not true during the latter 20th century. A third of the nation's welfare recipients now live in California. The state has the highest homeless population in the nation (135,000). About 22 percent of the nation's total homeless population resides in the state — whose economy is the largest in the U.S., fueling the greatest numbers of American billionaires and high-income zip codes."

Hanson goes on to explain how diseases are breaking out as *"typhus, along with outbreaks of infectious hepatitis A, are in the news on California streets. The sidewalks of the state's major cities are homes to piles of used needles, feces, and refuse."*

Instead of being part of the solutions, Professor Hansen writes, *"high-tech does its part not to clean the streets but to create defecation apps that electronically warn tourists and hoi polloi how to avoid walking blindly into piles of sidewalk excrement. In Californian logic, public defecation butts up against progressive tolerance, so it is exempt from the law. Yet, for a suburbanite to build a patio without a permit, for example, costs one dearly in fines. Indeed, a new patio without a permit can be deemed more dangerous to public health than piles of excrement in the public workplace."*

On lawlessness, he writes, *"Crime during the last three years has increased. It is an epidemic in local jails. San Francisco has the highest property-crime rate per capita of any major city. The California prison system is a mess, and sanctuary cities ensure that illegal aliens charged with crimes will not be deported."*

Pointing out that although California has the highest amount of sales, gas, and income tax, the state is now eyeing *"a punitive new inheritance tax, and it just imposed an Internet sales tax."*

California Governor Gavin Newsome responded after reading Victor Davis Hanson's brilliant article, by granting free health care to illegals ages 18–26. Again, it's the top dog that determines who gets what and who doesn't. But the drill down from *free* always results in the opposite of what these Socialists call *social justice.*

What's lacking in any debate as to why Socialism doesn't work is the answer to the question, *how are your policies different from what is going on in California?*

Jonathan, Victor Davis Hanson is incredible in that he boils it down to a level anyone with an I.Q. in a positive number can understand. Unfortunately, my friend Stephanie is below the minimum required level of comprehending what socialism does. Her response to what I read her was, **"Well, this time, it will be different."**

The fallacies of her and other socialists' thoughts are never exposed. The drill down to the facts results in a common response from those who cannot respond. They defer, deflect, and point the finger at someone else.

Bernie Sanders uses the Finland model of healthcare as the template for Medicare for all in this country. The logic fails from the standpoint when drilling down on all the variables of the U.S. vs. Finland, such as population size, ethnicity percentage, illegal immigration, free market vs. statist government, it fails at the very roots. A Statist government has the belief that the state should control either economic or social policy, or both, to some degree. **Why is Bernie or any of the Socialists in our government going to the Finland healthcare model when right here in the States we have a perfect example of what he wants...CALIFORNIA!**

That's a history you will never hear in the schools, by the mainstream media or the radical wing that now controls the Democratic Party. It's a coordinated effort of continued misinformation that bombards us daily with the purpose of controlling our minds to a belief that there is only one side to any argument. Whether it's Trump-Russia Collusion, the #MeToo movement, open borders, free health care, free college education, tax the evil rich to pay for everything, keep the status quo that gives the deep state power it achieved through one tactic...misinformation. A false fact is then repeated to the umpteenth time where fiction becomes fact, and those who believe otherwise are labeled with hateful names.

Jonathan, the current form of social disorder those in power use to control has its roots in community organizing in our country that comes from one person—Saul Alinsky. It's a repeated theme throughout the book and in our day to day lives.

Chaucer once said, *"All good things must come to an end,"* and they did with Stephanie. The final straw was when my illustrator, Galih, and I colluded to dump her in a manner causing less pain to me. I realized that there are more important things than being around a beautiful girl. As shallow as I've been in the past, I understood what you see on the outside isn't as important as a person's heart and mind. I drew from my past to compare her idol, Alexandria Ocasio-Cortez to Carmen Miranda (a Portuguese-born Brazilian samba singer, dancer, Broadway actress, and film star who was popular from the 1930s to the 1950s). Miranda was known for her fruit hat outfits.

The word *"broad"* is like a 4-letter word in Stephanie's PC, safe space world. But the fact was Stephanie lived like a gutter rat. No manners, burping all the time, dressing like a slob, never cleaning a dish, trash all over the place, and never seeing a toilet worth flushing. Good riddance, and as Sinatra brilliantly sang, *"That lady is a tramp!"*

The echo chamber of repeated words spew in unison from the MSM including, but not limited to, *"unconstitutional acts, disgrace, mentally unstable, fabricated crisis, collusion, obstruction, racist, homophobe, masochist, sexist, Hitler like, Authoritarian, a despot, shithole (referring to Trump's reference of Haiti), indictment, impeachment, 25th amendment, crimes, in crisis, felonies, etc."* continue as facts be dammed.

After almost three years of spewing Alinsky-like fear, they have no record of showing where they have been successful in their hateful messages. Unfortunately, there are those who only get one side of the story and never factor in those with differing opinions.

We must always remember, as Ronald Reagan once said:

Jonathan, I just gave the readers *fake news* as the speech was from October 27, 1964, at the Republican National Convention. It was Jeff Zucker, President of CNN Worldwide, who pointed this out to me. Thanks, Jeff, for finally getting something right.

Chapter 28

Always Remember and Never Forget

The message of *Never Forget* rings loudly as throughout the 20th century, over 125 million souls were lost due to their own leaders' murderous acts. These individuals ruled under Fascism, Socialism/Marxism, and Communism monikers. Despite the passing of time and with it generations who suffered despicable acts at the hands of tyrants whose governments persecuted their own people, the one thing that **keeps history alive is our first amendment right of Freedom of Speech.**

It's when those who speak the loudest—instead of the majority—try to destroy the history of our country by pulling in the past historical figures to today's standards, that history is lost. The same song Kate Smith sang in the 1930s as Paul Robeson, was the reason the New York Yankees pulled after decades Smith's rendition of God Bless America. The same forces (i.e., Colin Kaepernick), who object to a historic flag of Betsie Ross's flag on Nike sneakers, get the company to stop selling shoes that honor our country's history. An individual who doesn't even vote, the most fundamental right of any American, is called a social justice warrior. You only can judge individuals in the time they existed, not by modern standards as the only mark they left are their history. Not a revisionist history to obliterate what they stood for in their time.

In Kareem Abdul Jabbar's book, *Standing on the Shoulders of Giants,* in the introduction, he states, *"History is a living road map that allows us to see where others have been, what mistakes they've made and how we can avoid the same mistakes ourselves. Even better, we also see what others have done well and embrace their triumphs. We can let their accomplishment inspire us to be greater."*

As the present time becomes history, we are at an inflection point as the biggest attempt by members of our own government and their deep state players, along with other foreign governments have colluded to keep their power, preventing real justice from being served.

The greatest tragedy is the opportunity lost. If Julian Assange is not granted immunity to testify as to all he knows, the deep state operatives will be in control of the narrative. How convenient was it that Assange was silenced just before the Mueller report pointing the finger at him and WikiLeaks colluding with Russia to ensure a Trump election?

Mueller and his deep state operatives need to be held accountable for their actions and lack of them. As a great Cuban Band Leader would say:

But Jonathan, fate intervened, and it didn't take Ricky Ricardo to stop Mr. Mueller from riding off in the sunset as he announced during his retirement speech from the Justice Department on May 29th, 2019. During the House hearings on July 24th, 2019, with Mueller as the only witness, it was obvious that he lacked the fundamental information in the report that bore his name. Mueller, an undisputed Vietnam War hero, was now a puppet to the puppet master, Andrew Weissmann. Mueller's testimony revealed just how lacking he was in the information contained in the report and his lack of hands-on in micromanaging his prosecutors.

Even more shocking, **Mueller never heard of Fusion GPS or Glenn Simpson, who funded the Steele Dossier (with the DNC and the Clinton campaign).** It was Simpson who met with the Russian lawyer in the Trump Tower meeting before and after this arranged meeting to "*offer dirt on Hillary Clinton.*" Mueller's investigation made that meeting a significant part of the report. **It was the Steele Dossier that kicked off the phony FISA warrants into Carter Page, and with that, eventually, an investigation (Mueller) into no crime.** But again, **Glenn Simpson and Fusion GPS, the instigators were nowhere to be found in the Mueller Report.**

Mueller didn't even know until after he hired Jeanne Rhee that she served as Clinton's attorney on the FBI email investigation. He found about that later. However, Rhee remained on as a lead prosecutor.

After the hearing and Robert Mueller's reluctant testimony that was pushed by House chair, Jerrold Nadler, many questioned Mueller's past, and how much of a puppet he was for the deep state when he served as FBI Director. **The hearing on July 24ᵗʰ, 2019, will go down in history as the start of the crumbling of the deep state from within.** It's hard to feel sorry for Robert Mueller being used by Weissman, as the lives his special counsel destroyed will never fully be restored.

At the hearing, despite trying to be propped up by those who hate Donald Trump, even to a Close Minder, it was difficult to watch a man who appeared at times dazed, confused, and uncomfortably numb. As deep state as Bob Mueller might have been in prior scandals, his time has passed, and this hearing revealed how deeply disturbing Andrew Weissmann led a *no holds bar* effort to oust Donald Trump as President was. The fact that Nadler, Schiff, Weissmann, and his team even permitted Mueller from testifying, knowing his lack of knowledge and something, although I'm not a doctor, where he just mentally wasn't up to the job, shows you how the deep state will throw their young (in this case their old) to the wolves only to perpetuate a myth and keep their power.

History again is our guide. After President John F. Kennedy was assassinated on November 22nd, 1963 in Dallas, Texas, the biggest tragedy afterward was the conspiracy theories that ran rampant. If Lee Harvey Oswald had not been killed by Jack Ruby on November 24th, 1963 at the Dallas Police Station, history would not have been denied the opportunity to see what really transpired. Instead, President Kennedy's short legacy had more attention taken away from his accomplishments as human curiosity is more focused on myth than reality. The fascination with conspiracy theories involved Lyndon Johnson, the CIA, Raul Castro, Ted Cruz's father (just joking), etc. More documentaries focused on the assassination than Kennedy's accomplishments.

If Julian Assange is not allowed the freedom to tell us what happened, the truth will be forever lost to time. The deep state players and the MSM would have prevailed in polluting the narrative of Trump-Russia misdeeds, as it never existed in a world they have created for the Closed Minders and Oblivions. Additionally, there would be no reason for the MSM to expose the hoax they perpetrated on the American public.

If Barr too fails to prosecute the four individuals (Comey, McCabe, Rosenstein, and Yates) who all signed an illegal FISA warrant using the Steele Dossier violating Carter Page's 4th Amendment rights and only issues a judgment that the FISA process needs to be changed, the Deep State would have prevailed. As a skeptic, it's difficult to believe that Comey or Yates will be charged only because it brings it one step away from Loretta Lynch and Barack Obama. If justice is not upheld, stories will continually be perpetuated despite the fact they go far out of the realm of reality.

Sadly, even if Assange is granted his freedom, speculation runs rampant as to his physical and mental state.

There are so many evil people who have no interest in Julian Assange ever being set free:

1. Within the United Kingdom, it was a former British MI6 agent, Christopher Steele, who created the Dossier and this plot to destroy Donald Trump, a man he couldn't stand. Director Robert Hannigan, of the GCHQ (Government

Communications Headquarters) agency, gathered information secretly listening in to phone conversations, satellite signals, and reading e-mails. This agency decoded messages, monitored communication between people, and also made sure the Government's secrets were well kept. Coincidently, Mr. Hannigan resigned from this intelligence agency three days after President Trump took office on January 23rd, 2017.

2. Then, in our country, the *industrial-militaristic complex* despises Assange, as exposing crimes of the U.S. Military in Afghanistan and Iraq only goes to denigrate the image those in the military portray. Although a believer in a strong military as Ronald Reagan once said, *"There are some who've forgotten why we have a military. It's not to promote war, it's to be prepared for peace."*

Those who are whistleblowers and serve to expose crimes or differ with the groupthink mentality against the industrial-militaristic complex are taken out as Julian Assange has been...and Lt. Michael Flynn...and Paul Robeson...and those through our history who dared to stand up for their convictions.

Since his arrest by the UK Police on March 4th, 2019, Julian Assange has been silenced. It's best for those deep state operatives never to have their crimes exposed. Chances are, given all the U.S. and foreign government sabotage and crimes, he may never see the light of day. He **is literally the** *Man Who Knew too Much.*

Much like **Jeffrey Epstein**, who allegedly *"committed suicide"* on the morning of August 10th, 2019, the odds of Assange seeing the light of day and being able to speak out publicly are minimal, to say the least. When you know too much, it doesn't matter if in life you are a truth seeker or in Epstein's case, a disgusting human being. There are forces out there who rule us in the dark of night or in Epstein's case, in the light of the morning.

From Hitchcock's 1956 classic starring Jimmy Stewart and Doris Day, Assange has replaced Stewart as a deep state target. Stewart was not only a great actor but also a great American who was a fighter pilot in WWII. Doris Day was a nice lady whose lifetime achievements were marked beautifully after her acting career, showing a tremendous amount of love for our 4-legged creatures.

Whatever your political or emotional beliefs are, there are those on both sides of the fence who cherish our First Amendment rights. Those who seek to destroy it, whether it's the Soros-backed Antifa or the White Nationalists who seek to eliminate speech of those they disagree with, **the core value of Freedom of Speech is at the foundation of our existence as a Republic. True Americans at least agree on that fundamental right.**

The one common thread of all Americans is the mantra of the 1st Amendment, guaranteeing our right to speak our mind no matter what your beliefs are. In the *National Socialist Party of America vs. Village of Skokie, 432 U.S. 43 (1977),* the Supreme Court ruled in favor of freedom of speech and freedom of assembly. A Neo-Nazi group was granted their constitutional rights of freedom of speech and assembly if they did it in a peaceful manner. The Skokie Affair ruling became the landmark decision in granting any group the right of peaceful and free speech.

Julian Assange is hated by those he exposed and those who earn their power and wealth from making sure their crimes are not exposed. With that hate comes the repeated mantra to destroy his reputation, whether it be the alleged sexual crimes, *he's a narcissist, he's a liar*, it doesn't matter what they throw at him as the more you *"kill the messenger,"* the more you destroy his credibility.

Individuals who got caught red-handed committing crimes that would have never seen the light of day if Clinton was President would have a problem in Assange coming forth and testifying.

Religion, media, science, law, education, health, and technology are now controlled by those who show the most radicalism and outrage. What has been lost in this effort to destroy our Constitutional Rights is its victims.

Louis Brandeis, an Associate Justice on the Supreme Court, once said, *"To declare that in the administration of criminal law the end justifies the means, to declare that the Government may commit crimes in order to secure conviction of a private criminal would bring terrible retribution."*

Whether it's our government during the *Red Scare* or the *Mueller Special Counsel*, the Alinsky tactics illustrated in this book by the MSM and its allies only go to destroy the very fabric of our existence...the Constitution of the United States.

The *Red Scare* cost many their livelihoods. From after WWII to the time the McCarthy hearings were televised from April–June 1954, a sweeping effort on one side was made to condemn those who *allegedly* had ties to Communism. Blacklisting of individuals destroyed the lives of many in the entertainment media, including a who's who list of actors, actresses, entertainers, writers, and many common folks. Individuals' civil rights were denied.

Similar tales can be told by those who faced the full weight of the U.S. Government in the Mueller Investigation. Although history has shown the *Red Scare* as a black mark in our country's history, there are still many who control our thought processes who refuse to see the Mueller Special Counsel was an attempt to obstruct from bringing to justice those in our Government from a prior administration who broke the law repeatedly.

If the Assange truth does come out, justice will be served with the two-tier system of justice coming down as the deep state will be beaten to a pulp. But common sense says the numerous lawbreakers in attempting a coup will be so insulated from true justice as that is what power and money can do.

But in any event, here are my wishes:

I can only hope that Alcatraz will reopen as home to those who perpetrated the greatest coup in our country's history.

Julian Assange will have a major role in intelligence agencies overseeing, with proper checks and balances, our agencies no longer go rogue.

Barack Obama's Presidential Library will open...but not in this country.

Jonathan, Sandy the Squirrel, from SpongeBob Square Pants, was your first love.

Jonathan: *Dad, I miss her. She was special. But Transformers needed me more. Like you, I must save the world from evil and work with Optimus Prime to accomplish that feat.*

History will judge Donald Trump for his actions and not the malice shown against him as he dared to stand up against those who felt their power, wealth, and control over all of us was more important than our constitutional rights.

Schools will stop brainwashing our children and give them both sides of the story.

Walter Cronkite will no longer be spinning in his grave but will rest comfortably for eternity, knowing our Republic will survive and prosper.

What Julian Assange brings to the table is that he's the only individual who can blow up the deep state, the socialists/globalists, and the MSM that pushed the narrative of Trump-Russia Collusion. Without his testimony, our country will be locked up in a debate that will dampen the legacy of a President who never desired what these players did to him or the unsuspecting public.

Having a fresh face, Assange, who has never been proven wrong, injected with the volumes of reports exposing the real crimes of the deep state, will only get more Americans to pay attention as to why voting matters. An animal is most dangerous when it's wounded, and that's what the investigations initiated by Bill Barr hopefully will result in. The final blow of putting these despicable individuals out of power once and for all is Julian Assange, who will finally put them out of their misery. A Hillary Clinton presidency would have buried the deep state's misdeeds and only continued the status quo of criminal activity from within.

Jonathan, this book is about our country and its foundation stemming from the Constitution of the United States and its Bill of Rights. I could hide behind my disability or the fact I'm a senior citizen to fend off attacks by those who seek to destroy. A short time ago, we had a President who if you criticized him, you were labeled a racist by his proponents. He was insulated from attack only because he was black, and our country had a history that enslaved and treated those of color not with the respect all Americans are due. Hiding behind my age and my disability will never be my defense...as I will find another excuse to hide behind.

This book is about the history of our country, the Americana that is *The Good, Bad and Ugly.* Those who seek to eliminate history so they can spin a new narrative that fits their cause need to be held accountable to the facts and not the delusion they created that causes harm to the very foundation of our country...The Constitution.

There are individuals who will be so pissed off by what I've written, and there's a possibility that frivolous lawsuits against my imagination will be filed. But those individuals who do so have enough real legal problems to contend with that I will be the last on their list.

Also, caricatures of famous and infamous people used were not for the purpose of selling books but to make a point that these living and nonliving individuals created history that bears a valuable lesson for our present and possibly our future. ***As the Most Trusted Man in the Country*** Walter Cronkite once said, ***"In seeking truth, you have to get both sides of a story."*** This book gives all generations of Americans and welcomed legal immigrants to our country a vision of what a shining city on the hill could be once again.

Jonathan, truthfully, it doesn't matter to me what these anti-American, muckraking, law breaking, colluding, polluting, deluding, puking, Socialists/Globalists/Marxists trash, Constitutional smashing, thrashing, bashing, deep state cashing a_oles do or say as once an American icon said:

This book illustrates why our 1ˢᵗ Amendment rights are critical to the survival of our country. **Winston Churchill** once said, *"Some people's idea of free speech is what they are free to say what they like, but if anyone says anything back, that is an outrage."*

As Fox Mulder, Special FBI Agent from the X Files, once said:

It's not too late for someone who is a purveyor of the truth to tell us how screwed up our system really is. The deep state needs to be fully exposed, and with it, the power structure within our country that allowed them to get away with their crimes.

This is the time we all must care enough, and have the conviction and passion for standing up against all that seek to destroy bringing truth and equal justice to all. Until we see those who participated in the crimes outlined in this book brought to justice, the system has failed and emboldens the lawbreakers to continue their assault on our Constitution and our Bill of Rights.

Chapter 29

References and Acknowledgments

My Asperger's—Although I tend to live in my own world, I have an uncanny ability of focusing on a very narrow range of topics phasing out real-life experiences of most people. It's this narrow, intense ability to see reality, instead of using emotions, that provided the content in this book. It's a blessing and a curse, but as I revealed in my second book, *Dad, Why Are You So Weird?*, late in life, I used my limitations to live in a manner where most times, I'm happier than I've ever been.

This book might take me out of my old world into the unknown. My preference would have been to stay in my old world, as only during the last few years, I have begun to enjoy my life. However, I created for myself my country before privacy in the world. I sat down with Moe and Maisy and explained the sacrifices their fore doggies made for this country. They are both patriotic with Moe, like George. M. Cohan, born on the 4th of July. If Moe could speak, he would tell me, *"Dad, if you must leave, you must. Winston Churchill once said, "I was only the servant of my country and had I, at any moment, failed to express her unflinching resolve to fight and conquer, I should at once have been rightly cast aside."*

No one could ever imagine how difficult it is to place myself in a foreign, unknown world I've avoided my whole life. Asperger's separates my world from those of most. Although I'm a speck in time, it's my anger that has made me come out of the closet requesting to be heard.

As Howard Beale (aka Albert Finney) screamed a film classic line in the 1976 movie *Network*:

Beale, even in his outrage, knew of the evils of Russia, exclaiming, *"I don't know what to do about the depression and the inflation and the Russians and the crime in the street."*

Even decades before the deep state Mueller Report, a fictional character in 1976, like the Beav in 1960, Beale knew of Russians *and their evil ways.* Then there was the 1966 classic movie *The Russians Are Coming.* Folks the fact is the Russians have been coming a long time, but not in support of Donald Trump and his associates.

Moe, the Chihuahua—Taught me not to put up with anyone's bullshit and go for the jugular. In Moe's case, he goes for the ankles.

Thotiana—My muse, who not only took my verbal abuse in good stride but also suffered irreparable damage to her mind caused by my rationality. As she voted for Barack Obama twice, it was a difficult task to undo what she saw as the logic imparted on her that defied what the MSM and deep state only wanted her to believe.

However, truth be told, her brain survived mainly due to her constant use of marijuana. She had to be drugged up to be around me,

...but it was her own choice long before I met her. Eventually, she was able to see the light of truth at the end of the tunnel instead of what she was programmed to think.

Saul Alinsky—Unfortunately, he has never been given the credit he deserves for trying to work within the system to destroy our Constitution. His son, L. David Alinsky, said in an August 30th, 2008 piece in the Boston Globe, *"Barack Obama's training in Chicago by the great community organizers is showing its effectiveness. It is an amazingly powerful format, and the method of my late father always works to get the message out and get the supporters on board. When executed meticulously and thoughtfully, it is a powerful strategy for initiating change and making it really happen. Obama learned his lesson well."*

President Donald Trump*—Winston Churchill said in a speech before Parliament and over the radio on August 21st, 1940, as the Brits were in a battle for their lives, *"Never in the field of human conflict was so much owed by so many to so few."

Whatever motivations he had in being our President, the one that prevailed over all was his love for this country as witnessed by countless recordings over the decades as to the passion he showed when talking about the direction (or misdirection) the country was headed in. His family, too, has suffered, as no Presidential family has in our history been as brutally savaged by the MSM and other instigators of hate.

Thank you, Mr. President, for standing up to those whose only objective was to destroy what true Americans view as the basis of our country...The Constitution. Having been placed in a situation where you are surrounded by deep state operatives, I pray that you recognize those who protect individuals who committed obvious crimes from those whose only crime was exposing the Deep State. **Mr. President, it's important to remember our history and that of Wernher von Braun.**

The Constitutionalists—A core group of go-to people when looking at our Constitutional rights. Their intellect is off the charts. A heartfelt thanks to Thomas Sowell, American Economist and Social

Theorist who is currently a Senior Fellow at the Hoover Institution, Alan Dershowitz, Andy McCarthy, former U.S. Attorney for the Southern District Court of New York, Victor Davis Hanson, Ph.D. Sr. Fellow, Hoover Institution, Jonathan Turley, former Assistant U.S. District Attorney, Victoria Toensing and former U.S. District Attorney, Joseph DiGenova and Larry Sabato, Professor at University of Virginia and Founder and Director of the Center of Politics. To all of those who stood up for the foundation of our country's existence, The Constitution of the United States, a heartfelt thank you.

A special shout out to Victor Davis Hanson, a fellow Californian, whose level of common sense would make Thomas Paine and the Cleaver Family very proud. The Trump Administration should create a Department of Common Sense with Victor Davis Hanson as its Director.

Mark Levin's writings and his screeching voice show a passion unequaled for upholding Constitutional law. After reading a couple of pages of his books, I need to give my brain a rest. Brilliant mind.

Sorry CNN's legal analyst, Jeffrey Tobin. The numerous times I've seen you espousing your Trump *impeachment* rhetoric with no basis in law and more to your emotions, I needed that to obtain the balance on the other side to see the truth. However, to your credit, on a couple of occasions, you accidentally praised President Trump.

CNN's Jim Acosta—A perfect example of media bias as Acosta only uses emotions and a perverted logic to sell his views. Whatever happened to those reporters in the field who gave impartial views and were reporting the news instead of hate?

How perfect is it that in red on **his book cover** the title reads, ***Enemy of the People,*** then a bit lower in red it says, ***Jim Acosta?*** It probably would have been less funny if his editors added by his name, *by.* Thanks for exposing who you really are, Jimmy boy.

Judicial Watch through their FOIA (Freedom of Information Acts) requests has played a significant role in exposing the deep state and the abuses of the Obama Administration. Only one paragraph of thanks in this book, but much of the content revealed in this book is due to their efforts. Undying gratitude to Tom Fitton and Chris Farrell as much of what has come out would still be hidden from the public.

CNN & MSNBC—You need to see the whole picture, whether you agree or disagree with what they are espousing, to truly find what really occurred. The irony was it was the free MSM coverage that went to Trump rallies publicizing his candidacy that was the most significant part of why he was put in a position to beat out 16 Republican candidates and then Hillary Clinton. Their free coverage was the match for Hillary Clinton's campaign spending over $1 billion more that leveled the playing field and provided the impetus to have Donald Trump elected President. I guess as the views they espouse are supportive of Socialism/Marxism, bottom line it's the bottom line they were looking at. Thank you for your capitalistic impulses.

To Rachel Maddow. She puts the Kennedy assassination conspiracist theorists to shame. She is one of the go-to people as far as seeing how MSM looks to everything and the groupthink mentality. No one is better at spinning an intriguing yarn that is better found in a fairytale book than on cable news.

Personally, I find her quite attractive, both mentally and physically...only if she played for the other team. If she did, our nights would be full of lively conversation. If our brains didn't explode from fusing radical atomic nuclei, our later night activities would surely cause us to combust into another stratosphere spontaneously. Thank god for our first amendment rights. However, how ridiculous it is when people only look to one side of the story. Here's hoping one day Maddow opens the Alinsky School of Performing Arts Center.

To those brave to break from the MSM mentality that earned them a living: Greg Greenwald, attorney and ardent supporter of our 1st Amendment rights who frequently appeared on MSNBC, Sharyl Attkisson, former host of CNN Newsroom, and Lara Logan, longtime CBS Correspondent. Not easy going against your friends. Thank you.

Zerohedge.com—This site also provided the day-to-day minutia that pulled everything together for me and gave me the ability to sort out the truth.

SeekingAlpha.com—Since September 2014, I've been writing articles on two stocks (World Wrestling Entertainment and Cloudera). It was the editors at S.A. who gave me the ammunition to understand how to write my stories better.

Shawn Hannity—Was on the story before anyone and showed with the help of many, how corrupt our government was in trying to prevent Trump from becoming President, and afterward, trying to overthrow a duly elected President. Hannity always let the facts speak for themselves, and whatever the issue, he found the facts first before literally throwing these criminals behind bars. The MSM only continues the narrative against Hannity, Levin, Limbaugh, Ingraham, Carlson, and others outside the MSM that this is a *"right-wing conspiracy"* as touted by Hillary Clinton back in the day when Bill was attacked on whatever issue.

Truthfully, Hannity would have been next to my dog, Moe, in the credits, as an inspiration and truth seeker. But the MSM would have destroyed my narrative labeling me *a right-wing conspirator.* Therefore, I buried him deep in the acknowledgment section.

The past couple of years, Hannity has been *"peeling the onion back one layer at a time,"* on the greatest political coup in our country's history. It's time to take a machete and cut the onion in half. The American people need to shed a tear for what could have happened but for the bravery of those who dared to stand up against groupthink. This is a shout out to Danny Trejo, who uses that hand tool to destroy evil.

Sarah Carter and John Solomon—Both of *The Hill* with Carter eventually becoming a Fox Correspondent. These guys are the Woodward and Bernstein of our time, disclosing narratives that ran counter to what the MSM espoused. They will never win a Pulitzer like Woodward and Bernstein did for *All the Presidents Men* for they are on the wrong side of the MSM. Instead, reporters who perpetuated the hoax were awarded Pulitzers.

The Freedom Caucus in the House of Representatives including Devin Nunes, Ron DeSantis (now governor of Florida), Jim Jordan, and Mark Meadows; others including Representatives Louis Gohmert, Doug Collins, Matt Gaetz, John Ratcliffe, Louie Gohmert, and Jason Chaffetz; and those who dared to speak out in the Republican party. These individuals resisted the opposition on both sides of the political spectrum and tried to get the truth out. Unfortunately, it took several years to show what they knew and said was true. It's always difficult when there is a *kill the messenger* mentality by those who hate a President and the Constitution.

The Charles Barkleys of the world, who speak their minds without reservations despite the ramifications. On top of that, he's truly funny. He is a great HOF basketball player who should also go in the People's HOF, as he calls them as he sees them.

Kimberley Strassel, Wall Street Journal Editorial Board, and Catherine Herridge, a Fox News Correspondent. There are some journalists, not many, who verify facts before reporting a story. These two ladies are part of old-style journalism.

Geraldo Rivera, who always was a truth-seeker, only I don't always agree with him.

Former Secret Service Agent, Dan Bongino, who is as straight a shooter as there ever was.

Sebastian Gorka, an immigrant from Hungary who understands *"Why We Fight."*

To many others whose voices would not be silenced, including Dennis Praeger, Bill O'Reilly, and Dennis Miller. A special thanks to the late Alan Colmes, Charles Krauthammer, and Tim Russert.

Senator Lindsay Graham—Viewed mostly as a shadowy figure and puppet to John McCain. What emerged after McCain passed was someone who will fight to uphold the Constitution. It really surprised me as to how strong he is in defending individuals' constitutional rights, starting with the Judge Kavanaugh hearing, and now with his determination to get to the bottom of an attempted *coup d'état.*

To the Fox Business Network and their stalwart lineup of people who sought the truth, including Maria Bartiromo, Stuart Varney, Lou Dobbs, Neil Cavuto, Charles Payne, and Trish Regan. Maria, Stuart, Lou, and Neil have been part of my must-see TV business over the decades. The same for Joe Kernen and David Faber on CNBC. Thanks to CNBC's Rick Santelli and Steve Liesman, as I really enjoy seeing both of you go at it. Thanks to Rick for being the genesis of the Tea Party movement and financial responsibility. A shout out to legends of investment world Louis Rukeyser and John Bogle...although gone, they will never be forgotten.

To the upcoming generations, including Candace Owens, Ben Shapiro, Tami Lahren, Katie Pavlich, Charlie Kirk, Caitlin Johnstone, and the list goes on. It's up to this generation to ensure and offset the Globalist/Socialist cabal that's trying to make us all the same. It's not out of the realm of probability that Candace Owens will someday be President of the United States. A brilliant mind who won't back down and gives me tremendous hope to future generations who support our freedoms under the Constitution of the United States. Truly a remarkable crop of up and coming young people. On Caitlan, whatever her political leanings are, she's right on with Julian Assange.

To James O'Keefe of Project Veritas, who exposes those who seek to control, going undercover and getting the manipulators to freely offer information as to how they do what they do.

To the 1950s and early 1960s television including *Get Smart, Leave it to Beaver, Father Knows Best, The Ozzie and Harriet Show, The Donna Reed Show,* and one very few people (who are alive) will recall, *Fractured Flickers* (1963-1964). Starring voiceover legend, Hans Conried, *Fractured Flickers* showcased Conried's off-the-wall comedy, setting up old-time newsreels and scenes from old movies edited to bring you to a Mad Magazine level of entertainment. The inspiration for this long-forgotten show was the basis of how I used my illustrator Galih's incredible artwork to make a point.

Don Rickles, the King of Insults, known by the younger generation as the voice of Mr. Potato Head in Toy Story, made fun of all—where it didn't matter your color, religion, age, sex, or how you look. His logic was people are people, and we need to laugh. I never heard a bad word said about this comedy legend. A Don Rickles could not exist in today's PC culture. **As Jerry Seinfeld put it on why he won't play colleges anymore,** *"They just want to use these words: That's racist; that's sexist; that's prejudice. They don't know what the hell they're talking about."*

To Larry David, who I consider the funniest person on the face of the planet. Classic *Curb Your Enthusiasm* Season 4, Episode 1 where Larry turns down sex with a very alluring woman after he sees she has a photograph of George W Bush. So much for his 10th Anniversary gift from his wife, Cheryl. Larry is a comedy icon, and I can only dream of reaching his heights. It won't happen as I'm only 5'4", and he's 6'3".

To Johnny Carson, the true King of Late Nite, there was a time when late nite meant *funny*.

My Brother David—He was once the only person who could argue with me on an even playing field. He is the most brilliant person I have ever known. His intellect took a nice downfall with President Obama's UN speech on September 23rd, 2009, that called for Israel to relinquish territory won in the 6-day war in 1967, and go back to those borders giving Palestinians their own state. When questioned, David said, *"Well, he made a mistake."* Please buy his book, *"Marriage in the Land of the Sheep's Head,"* but not until after you buy mine.

To all those individuals including, but not limited to, Carl Bernstein, Bill Kristol, Governor John Kasich, former Nixon counsel John Dean, MSNBC Hosts Mika and Joe, and all those who take their self-righteousness to the extreme to where the truth has no bearing to the facts as they try to stir up the emotions of the unexpecting to how evil Donald Trump is. As the public catches on, sinking ratings and popularity can become a bitch!

To Jon Stewart—Although we agree to disagree on many issues, your commitment and efforts to see the 9/11 First Responders are provided medical care and support deserves a sincere *Thank You*. Also, like me, Jon loves WWE.

Dinesh D'Souza—Knew the risks of going against Big Brother and the Obama Administration and paid the price.

To Howard Stern—Although you jumped the shark when you divorced your first wife, Allison, and married Beth, I loved listening to you when you were suffering just as much as I was in my marriage. You are a beacon of light to those who believe in the First Amendment.

To Randall Stevenson, CEO at AT&T. I have a large position in my retirement account in your company. Can you start again being the purveyor of the truth? Become true to the greatest voice of all time moniker for your network. Make James Earl Jones's words again, *The most trusted name in news* relevant and get rid of those (i.e., Jeff Zucker) who says it's his network's job to report what they believe to be true, instead of being investigators seeking the truth. Do Bernard Shaw and those journalists who came before justice to the profession...or at least try.

I'm especially saddened about George Will as his love of baseball and verbiage he uses to describe the game on Ken Burn's *Baseball* documentary was nothing more than majestic. However, as brilliant as he is, Will thinks what happened is politics as usual and misses the whole scenario of how the deep state and the socialist movement have overtaken the rule of law on so many fronts in their disinformation campaign at all levels.

To the ACLU—Where were you when individuals whose views you disagree with had their constitutional rights abused?

Keith Olbermann, a great sportscaster, who turned political hack big time. Stick to what you're good at. Hint: We both, as kids, collected baseball cards.

To Jeff Flake, Paul Ryan, and Mitt Romney, and many others in the establishment Republican Party. Start defending our Constitution, give up your righteous indignation, and call out those who were trying to overthrow a duly elected President.

Administrative Law Judge Eli Palomares—We've all had situations in court that we deemed unfair in its outcome. Being the older father of a special needs child/adult, my concerns for his wellbeing go far past the time I'm on the planet.

Unaccountable bureaucrats are given power without having to answer to gross willful negligence as there is no mechanism within the State of California Department of Social Services to hold them to the standard where abuses are addressed. This judge denied my son's and my constitutional rights of due process by ignoring indisputable facts and creating a scenario to deny services my son needs. I'm sure others have been victims of those who have no accountability within the web of bureaucracy across the country.

During an Administrative Hearing on April 16th, 2018, Judge Palomares based his decision to deny protective supervision services on evidence that was outdated, factually incorrect, and irrelevant, referring to a social worker's less than 10-minute observations over the final determination of over 45 hours of study from clinical psychology experts. This analysis included sit-downs with two Clinical Psychologist who affirmed that Jonathan needs 24/7 supervision to remain in a safe environment.

Judge, I wrote to you that I hope what you did to my son and me comes back to you, so you know how it feels. Now you know.

My father (real dad) taught me when someone knocks you down, you get up and give them twice what they gave you...or maybe that was Donald Trump or Sylvester Stallone (aka Rocky). In any case, as the Judge is an employee of the State, I emailed him a letter. In the letter, true to form, I explained the rationale for him to come to his decision:

"Either you are very incompetent or had a predisposed bias against me. Unfortunately, I believe the latter is true as it would have been self-evident even to one of the Three Stooges that what you wrote in your decision was pure bullshit!"

To those who love the Stooges like I do, I did not mean to put this *fake fact* judge in the same category as Curly, Larry, and Moe. But in any event, Judge Palomares is a knucklehead.

Books and Analysis:

Charles Ortel—Detailed audit from public information of the Clinton Foundation, showing it to be nothing more than a scam. With Asperger's, my affinity toward numbers shows this foundation never added up.

William Edward Binney, a former highly placed intelligence official with the United States National Security Agency, turned whistleblower. He retired on October 31, 2001, after more than 30 years with the agency. Much like Ortel's analysis, Binney's analysis is the definitive study showing that the DNC information was downloaded to a thumb drive, not hacked. It made sense when reading his analysis. Again, I'm a numbers person, and Mueller's Assange-Russian hacks never added up, if only because Julian Assange has never been caught in a lie, and nothing he has ever published has been disproven. To date, no one has debunked Binney's theory on the DNC info being downloaded to a thumb drive. The most likely reason it has never been analyzed is the writers of the books on the Trump-Russia Hoax do not have the technological background to understand what exactly transpired.

Greg Jarrett's—*The Russian Hoax: The Elaborate Scheme to Frame Donald Trump and Elect Hillary Clinton* should be textbook reading in schools in history classes, as he brilliantly reveals major crimes by those in power.

Peter Schweitzer—*Clinton Cash*—A detailed blow-by-blow analysis of *"Where there is smoke, there is fire."* The trail of deceit is only substantiated by Charles Ortel's physical audit of publicly released documentation on the Clinton Foundation.

Judge Janine Pirro—*Liars, Leakers, and Liberals*—Her understanding of the process where this corruption was parsed through all the top levels of government is attributed to her tremendous legal background.

Sydney Powell—*Licensed to Lie: Exposing Corruption the In Department of Justice* details the escapades of Andrew Weissmann and the prosecutorial abuses used in destroying the lives of innocent people. Weissmann and his prosecutors were responsible for bringing down Arthur Andersen, and with that, over 80,000 jobs. The Supreme Court eventually ruled against Weissmann and his attack dogs (9-0), reversing the prison conviction of top Arthur Andersen officers. The behaviors of Mueller and his team headed by Andrew Weissmann during the Trump-Russia Collusion investigation again mirror prosecutorial abuse exhibited in the past.

Seamus Bruner—*Comprised: How Money and Politics Drive FBI Corruption* details the crony capitalism Mueller and Comey have shown each other over the years.

To a legend in political cartoons, Paul Conrad enjoyed his political humor with the *L.A. Times* for decades.

The Mueller Report—To understand the truth, you must see how the story was put together in the first place. Mueller's report shows how people who didn't care about the truth only looked at what the *creators* of the Trump-Russian collusion threw out and not the actual evidence.

The Mueller timeline leaves out its most corrupt elements and how the government, through the Obama Administration and Hillary Clinton assets, used its full resources and power against individuals because of who they supported. Disgusting, to say the least.

Mueller investigators did not look into the roots of a counterintelligence investigation that has shown there was no collusion. It's like seeing someone shooting another person, then looking at what happened to the person who got shot without looking at the person who did the act. Despite being given wide discretion as witnessed by the Cohen and Manafort prosecutions, he chose not to look at the crimes committed, leading to his investigation.

Nothing proves Walter Cronkite's belief that you need two sides of the story to determine what is the truth, than the convenient omissions from the Mueller report of all the key actors performing espionage on behalf of the Obama Administration and key heads of our intelligence agencies.

Where are the key actors from the start in Mueller's report, including former British MI6 agent, Christopher Steele, who was funded by Fusion GPS, the DNC, and the Clinton surrogates? Logic states if you are going to investigate key individuals who are the main part of your report, why not go back to the start, and how it led up to it? Conspicuously absent from the Mueller Report are numerous individuals mentioned in this book. The good thing, in the end, was it only cost the American taxpayer $32 million. Well, not true as Rep Schiff and Nadler continue to spend our tax dollars looking for crimes.

To those I forgot to mention and are passionate about understanding the rule of law and how important our constitutional rights are—Keep up the good fight.

To the victims of the McCarthy Hearings—May God rest your souls. Your beliefs, whatever they were, should never have been used to destroy your lives.

To victims of the Mueller Investigation—May justice be served on those who committed real crimes not only against you but against our constitutional rights. May, as Spock so eloquently put it, *"You live long and prosper."*

Lt. General Michael Flynn should be given the Medal of Honor for how he stood tall against impossible odds.

To the British Invasion from Winston Churchill to Margaret Thatcher to the Stones and The Who to The Cure and all the past historical figures and incredible musical talents to the current groups who have had a positive impact on my life and millions of Americans.

To the younger generations—It's up to you to see reality as you need to look at both sides to see the truth. Eliminate emotion and fairly evaluate an issue important to our country by weighing the facts. If the facts don't add up to what you are told to believe, question the disseminator of the questionable facts and drill down.

Jonathan, life is mostly common sense. With any action, there is a predictable counter-reaction. **It's time good sense was exercised, and those who were a part of this coup d'état be held accountable for their crimes. If not, there is no such thing as equal justice for all, and our Constitutional rights will end up in the trash bin of history.**

Winston Churchill once said:

Finally, to my real parents, I couldn't have done it without you...as I wouldn't have been born.